CONTENTS

HORRIBLE HISTORIES

INCREDIBLE INCAS

Terry Deary Illustrated by Martin Brown & Philip Reeve

SCHOLASTIC

To Virginia Garrard-Burnett, who proposed this book and researched it.
Sincere thanks.

Scholastic Children's Books,
Euston House, 24 Eversholt Street,
London NW1 1DB, UK

A division of Scholastic Ltd
London ~ New York ~ Toronto ~ Sydney ~ Auckland
Mexico City ~ New Delhi ~ Hong Kong

First published in the UK by Scholastic Ltd, 2000
This edition published 2017

Text © Terry Deary, 2000
Cover illustration © Martin Brown, 2008
Inside illustrations © Philip Reeve, 2000

ISBN 978 1407 17866 0

Printed and bound by CPI Group (UK) Ltd, Croydon, CR0 4YY

4 6 8 10 9 7 5

The right of Terry Deary, Martin Brown and Philip Reeve to be identified as the author and illustrators of this work has been asserted by them in accordance with the Copyright, Designs and Patents Act, 1988.

www.scholastic.co.uk

Introduction

History can be horrible because history, like school, can be full of bullies ...

You'll be having a nice, peaceful life when along comes a bully and changes all that...

Who do you feel sorry for? The victim, of course!

But history is never that simple. Sooner or later the bully will meet up with an even more scary bully – usually one with better weapons...

Who do you feel sorry for now?

And what does the bully do when s/he's bullied? Give in and become a slave? Or stand up to the new bully?

The Incas were a bit like that. They came along and bullied the people of Peru into handing over their wealth. Then along came the Spanish invaders (the 'conquistadors') and turned the Incas into slaves.

So who do you feel sorry for?

To be honest there are no easy answers. That's why history is so horrible.

Of course school history books like questions with easy answers!

Question: 'When did the Spanish arrive in Peru?'

Answer: '1532.'

B-O-R-I-N-G!

But this is a horrible history and it will look at the questions that really matter. So trash that textbook and find out the terrible truth about the Incas …

Timeline

Early Incan timeline

11,000 BC The first people settle in the area we now call Peru.

1250 BC Tribes of people begin to form in the Andes. They're called things like Chavin and Chimu, Nazca and Tiahuanaco.

AD 600 For a couple of hundred years the people from the Huari region will boss the western Andes. With them comes the spread of mummy burial. (That's corpses wrapped in cloth, not burying your mother.)

900 The Huari have gone (in a bit of a Huari) and the people split into tribes again. Most of these little states are no bigger than a single valley.

1105 Around this time the first Incan lord, Sinchi Roca, begins to rule his tribe, but his people are not very powerful ... yet.

1370 The Chimu people are the biggest bullying bosses in Peru. They're led by Nancen Pinco who lives in Chan Chan. It seems as if these Chimu built a new palace for each new ruler and kept the old palaces going after the rulers died.

1438 The little Incan tribe starts to grow quickly and that means

trouble. Over the next fifty years the incredible Incas will conquer all the other tribes and rule them.

Incan Empire timeline

1100 The Incas start to spread out and conquer other people. Maybe a few years of dry weather left them low on food so they had to go out and pinch it.

1438 The Chanca people attack the Incas. They're defeated but the invasion starts the Incas fighting amongst themselves.

1492 Chris Columbus stumbles across America. He'll soon be followed by Spanish conquistadors who'll conquer the South American peoples. They haven't reached the Incan lands yet … but give them time.

1525 A terrible plague sweeps through the Incan homeland – probably a disease like measles or smallpox brought from Europe. The Spanish aren't in Peru yet but their germs are!

Later we'll see what happens when the Spanish arrive…

Legendary lords

Where do humans come from? People have wondered this since they had two brain cells to think with.

Scientists say . . .

They could be right.

Christians say…

They could be right. The Bible reckons God made us in his image and some of us are very god-like, aren't we?

But the Incas came up with an even more sensible idea…

A bit like worms!

Lord number 1: Mighty Manco

There are three caves at Paqari–tampu where (they say) the first Incan leader first saw the light of day. His name was Manco Capac and he popped out of one of the caves with his three brothers and four sisters. Ten groups of people appeared from the other caves, but naturally the Incas were the leaders. Then they set off on a great journey through the Andes…

THEY LOOKED FOR GOOD SOIL TO FARM AND GROW CROPS. MANCO HAD A BRIGHT IDEA…

MY BROTHERS EAT TOO MUCH! THERE'LL BE MORE FOOD FOR THE REST OF US IF I KILL THEM!

THAT'S WHAT HE DID. ONE WAS SEALED IN A CAVE AND TWO WERE TURNED TO STONE. THEN HE DID SOMETHING VERY STRANGE…

I NEED A WIFE. I CAN'T MARRY ONE OF THE COMMON PEOPLE. I'LL MARRY MY SISTER, MAMA OCLLO!

HELP!

IN TIME THEY HAD CHILDREN…

LET'S CALL THIS LITTLE CHAP SINCHI ROCA

AT LAST THE INCAS ARRIVED AT CUZCO.

SEEMS LIKE A NICE PLACE!

Incan legends say Manco was the first of eight Lords of Cuzco – their valley in the Andes. No one is sure how true the stories about the eight lords are. The important thing is that most Incas *believed* these stories.

Lord number 2: Super Sinchi

Another story says that when Manco Capac died there were lots of his children who could have taken his place. The people all wanted Sinchi Roca… but Sinchi was NOT expected to take the throne ahead of his brothers.

How did he do it? With a bit of help from his mum! Would you like to be the next Prime Minister/President/King/Queen of your country? Here's how Mama Ocllo fixed it for Sinchi…

The trick seemed to work and Sinchi Roca was made the new Lord of Cuzco.

Stylish Sinchi

Sinchi was much more peaceful than dead old Manco. He spent less time murdering people and more time inventing things. What was his greatest invention? It was something that would show all the people who the royal family were, at a glance.

What did super Sinchi invent?

a) golden crowns   **b)** purple robes   **c)** fringe hairstyles

Answer: **c)** Yes, Sinchi Roca said that the Incan rulers would have their hair cut straight across the forehead.

Sinchi Roca started another new trend after he died! He was the first of the Incan lords to be turned into a mummy. The corpse was kept so well it was put on show in Cuzco two hundred years after he died.

Lord number 3: Lovely Lloque

Third emperor (Lloque Yupanqui) was a pretty peaceful bloke compared to Manco. Even though he didn't go around flattening farmers, looting lands and ruling ruthlessly he was still remembered as . . .

Surprisingly enough, Lloque was called 'left-handed' because… he was left-handed.

Unforgettable? Well anyone who looked at Lloque would never forget him. That face would haunt your dreams for ever. He was simply the *ugliest* man anyone had ever seen! His sad story is soon told…

- People who saw him ran away.
- His chief wife couldn't stand the sight of him.
- He had no children with his chief wife.
- He was advised to take the daughter of a neighbouring chief for a wife – she couldn't stand the sight of him either.
- Her father forced her to marry Lloque and she gave birth to Mayta Capac.

Unforgettably ugly – do you know anyone like that?

Lord number 4: Mighty Mayta Capac

The fourth Lord of Cuzco, Mayta Capac, was big trouble from the moment he was born.

- Legend said that he was born six months before he was due.
- As a newborn baby he was strong and had all his teeth.
- By the time he was a year old he was as big as an eight-year-old. (Imagine the size of his nappies!)

Mayta ruled in the 1300s and began invading the tribes next to Cuzco valley. What was it that made Mayta such a nasty neighbour? The weather!

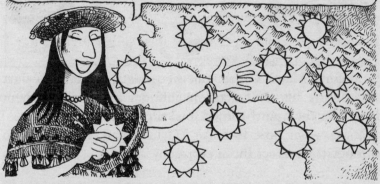

... AND DRY WEATHER IS FORECAST FOR THE NEXT FEW YEARS. CROPS WILL BE POOR, PEOPLE WILL STARVE AND WATER WILL BECOME PRECIOUS. OH, AND DON'T FORGET YOUR FACTOR 99 SUN CREAM IF YOU'RE GOING OUTSIDE! GOODNIGHT!

Mayta wasn't going to go hungry. He was simply going to train his people to fight and go out and pinch the food and water from other tribes. He was going to be the biggest bully since Manco Capac.

It's not surprising, really. Stories say Mayta had grown up as a big, bad boy, picking fights with any boys he came

15

across. (You probably know someone like that.) He wasn't afraid to fight with bigger boys and the legends say he 'beat them badly'.

While he was still a boy he picked a fight with some peasants near Cuzco and killed them. This started a revolt by their tribe and his dad had trouble keeping it under control...

So mighty Mayta Capac was the perfect emperor to start conquering his next-door neighbours and making them hand over their hard-earned food supplies.

It was soon time to make Mayta a man. He had to go through the correct Incan ceremony...

Bye-bye boyhood
Do you know anyone who is growing into a man? Then instead of a birthday party or a school-leaver's do, why not give them a special treat? An Incan initiation! Follow these simple Incan rules to see your pal safely into the adult world...

16

MAKING IT INTO MANHOOD
(How to turn a boy into a man.)

You need: a llama, a sharp knife, a whip, a running track, a sling, a shield, a hard wooden club (called a 'mace'), a hole punch, a breechcloth (like a big boy's nappy) — and don't forget the boy!

1. First sacrifice your llama. (Sneak up behind the llama with your club. Club it to death, skin it and roast the meat.)

2. Offer the meat to the god of the Sun.

YUM!

3. Strip the boy to the waist, give him the whip and let him whip himself to drive out his boyhood.

OW!
AGH! OUCW!
HOP IT, BOYHOOD!

4 Arrange a foot race around a running track so the new man can show his speed against the other men.

PUFF!
PANT!

5. Give the new man his weapons — a sling, a shield and a club.

OOH, TA!

(Wipe the llama's blood off the club before you present it.)

6. Pierce the new man's ears so everyone can see at a glance he is no longer a boy.

OW! ME EARS!

7. Give him his new name and his breechcloth.

17

Lord number 5: Conquering Capac

Mayta Capac made his son, Capac Yupanqui, Lord of Cuzco… then Mayta died. Most lords named their oldest son to be the next ruler. Young Capac Yupanqui *wasn't* Mayta Capac's oldest son. What was wrong with Capac Yupanqui's older brother?

a) he was too thick

b) he was too ugly

c) he was too kind and gentle

Answer: **b)** Yes, the poor lad took after his grandfather, Lloque, and was considered too ugly to be the Lord of the Incas. (Not like royals today! It seems they *have* to be ugly to get the job!)

Capac Yupanqui was the first Incan lord to capture lands outside the Cuzco Valley where the Incas started. But he only got about 12 miles from Cuzco. He wasn't exactly Julius Caesar or Alexander the Great, you understand.

Capac Yupanqui was known as the 'Unforgettable King' ... unfortunately we know very little about his reign. It seems that everyone has forgotten!

Lord number 6: Roca on – again!

Capac Yupanqui's son, Inca Roca, conquered a bit more to the south-east of Cuzco but the Incas weren't the greatest warriors, as the following story shows...

Lord number 7: Huacac whack, whack!

Yahuar Huacac couldn't have hated his Ayarmaca captivity that much. He married an Ayarmaca girl! But then he also married other wives. Not a very healthy thing to do. Today, in most countries, marrying two women will get you punished. But in Incan times it was more deadly.

Yahuar Huacac announced…

And, would you believe it, the second wife arranged for the second son of the first wife to be murdered.

This was followed shortly after by the emperor's own death…

Lord number 8: Vicious Viracocha

Viracocha probably ruled around the early 1400s. He wasn't satisfied with being a 'lord' – he called himself 'Creator God'. (This is a bit like your head teacher calling themselves Minister of Education. A teeny bit over the top.)

Before Vile Vira came on the scene the Incas had attacked other tribes, conquered them, then gone home. Now Vira decided it was time they stayed there and ruled. First they decided to take over the Ayarmaca people who lived to the south of the Incas' Cuzco valley. So what did they do?

Wrong! The Incas were smarter than you – that's why they got to rule Peru, which is more than you'll ever do. No, the Incas attacked the Urubamba! This was a valley beyond the Ayarmaca.

It worked. Whichever way the Ayarmaca faced they'd be stabbed in the back.

Evil emperors

The eight Incan lords had so far ruled only little Cuzco ... and if that had been the end of the story you'd probably never have heard of them. But then they became more and more greedy. They wanted more land, more wealth, more people to push around. They weren't happy with a valley, or even a country. They wanted a whole empire. And, it was the next Incan lord, a lad called Pachacuti, who was the man for the job.

Did you know...?
Pachacuti got his name after a great battle victory. 'Pachacuti' means 'cataclysm' – or 'he who shakes the Earth'.

COULD YOU STOP DOING THAT PLEASE?

Pachacuti's date with fate: 1438

The Incas didn't get all their own way in bossing the Andes. Another people, the Chancas, to the west of the Incas, were getting pretty powerful. In 1438 the Chancas attacked first!

The Lord of Cuzco's son, Pachacuti Inca Yupanqui, defended their Cuzco home while his dad, Viracocha, went off with his other son, Urcon, to a safer fort near Calca. Now there were *two* Inca states – Pachacuti's and Viracocha's. But not for long. First Viracocha died.

GLURK!

THANKS DAD, IT'S VERY THOUGHTFUL OF YOU!

Then Viracocha's other son Urcon got into a fight with Pachacuti's forces and was killed.

THANKS BROTHER, IT'S VERY THOUGHTFUL OF YOU!

It left Pachacuti in charge.

Pach's pinching

Pachacuti defeated the Chanca attack thanks to a bit of luck. The Chancas took an image of their god into battle and Pach's warriors managed to capture it. The Chancas panicked and began to run away. They were massacred. Pach made the most of this victory and told a bit of a fib to make it sound more magical…

THE CHANCAS STARTED TO RUN AWAY INTO THE HILLS. THEY MIGHT HAVE ESCAPED AND LIVED TO FIGHT AGAIN! BUT THE ROCKS OF THE HILLS TURNED INTO INCA WARRIORS. THE ROCKS CAUGHT THE CHANCAS AND CUT THEM TO PIECES. THE GODS LOVE THE INCAS AND TURNED THE ROCKS INTO SOLDIERS TO FIGHT FOR US!

A MIRACLE!

The truth? As the Chancas ran away hundreds of Inca supporters, living in the hills, ran down and attacked them. Yes – the Chancas were massacred in the hills. But, no – the attackers weren't rocks!

Terror tactics
Pachacuti's big fib was widely believed. Enemies of the Incas were scared and the Incan warriors made the most of that fear. This is what they did…

1 Incan armies started to carry platforms into battle. On these platforms were piles of sacred stones.

Future enemies took one look at the pile of Incan rocks and gave up without a fight!

2 To add to the fear-factor the Incas took the defeated Chanca leaders and stuffed their skins with straw and ashes. The scarecrow corpses were taken to a special burial ground and seated on stone benches. The stuffed arms were bent so

that when the wind blew the dead fingers beat the stretched skin on their bellies like drums! The message was clear...

3 The Incan warriors went into battle with war songs that were grisly and gruesome. Want to try one? Next time your history teacher gives you a dreadful detention then fight back with this ancient Incan chant...

We'll drink chicha from your skull
From your teeth we'll make a necklace
From your bones we'll make our flutes
From your skin we'll make a drum

Of course you couldn't *really* drink chicha from your teacher's skull because chicha is beer. You wouldn't want to get into trouble for under-age drinking, would you? Probably best if you just drink cocoa from the teacher's skull and stay out of trouble. (And no playing those bone flutes and skin drums when people are trying to get to sleep!)

Brotherly love

Pachacuti's warriors seemed unbeatable. The trouble was that Pach's younger brother, Capac Yupanqui, was having a great time invading neighbours and becoming a rich, powerful, popular general. Pach was worried.

What did he do? Well, if the Incas had a motto it would be, 'When in doubt, snuff them out!' So of course, Pachacuti had his brother murdered. Being the brother of an Incan emperor was a job for life – but sadly that life was often very short.

Pachacuti's sons went north and south conquering their neighbours and making the Incan Empire safe – safe for the Incas, that is.

Now Pachacuti could stop the fighting and enjoy a bit of ruling.

Pach's patch and Top Cat Topa
Pachacuti decided it was time for some changes and he had the power to make them. He had only taken over as emperor from his father after a lot of fighting and he didn't want that to happen when he died, so he made his son Topa Inca Yupanqui the next emperor, then retired.

Topa was topa the pops when it came to ruling and he and his dad made some nice new rules. If the Incas had been able to write, their laws may have read something like this…

THE TEN INCA COMMANDMENTS

1. Cuzco will be the capital of the Incan Empire. The fortress of Sacsahuaman in Cuzco will be the strongest in the world.

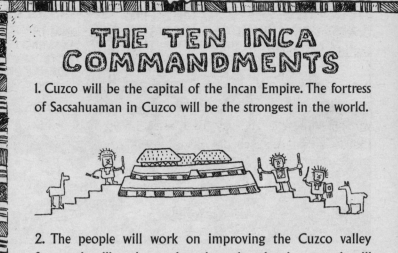

2. The people will work on improving the Cuzco valley farms – levelling the earth and moving the river – so it will be the greatest food producer ever.

3. A dead emperor's lands will be shared out amongst his family. Each new emperor must conquer new lands of his own.

4. Conquered peoples will be scattered round other parts of the Incan Empire to work for the Incas – that will also stop them gathering together to revolt.

5. Girls of conquered tribes may become Chosen Women (Quechua Aclla Cuna) to serve in the Incan temples or be married off to great Incan soldiers.

6. A number of conquered men will be chosen to serve in the Incan Army.

7. Everyone will worship the Incan god, Viracocha. There will be priests, prayers and temples. All conquered peoples must worship Viracocha, and pay his priests with food and work. (But they can keep their old religion too.)

8. The emperor may marry his sister, but no other men may marry their sisters.

9. The emperor may marry as many women as he wishes, but no other man may. A chief minister may have 50 wives, an ordinary minister just 30 and the lower your class the fewer wives you may have.

10. If anyone wishes to speak to the emperor then he or she must take off their sandals and place a small load on their back as a sign of respect.

Imagine that in your country! First you're invaded and then you're…

- Split from your friends – all those mates who share the same jokes and support the same football team.
- Split from your sisters who are sent off to work in some distant temple or forced to marry some great national hero … like Prince Charles!
- Forced to work to pay for food that mostly goes to your enemy … like a vegetarian working in a butcher shop.

- Shipped off to another part of the invader's world where you don't know the language and live in a strange house. It could be anywhere … like Bournemouth, Blackpool or Buckie!
- Taught a new religion with new prayers and forced to worship a new god. It's a bit like being forced to support a new football team … like Bournemouth or Blackpool or Buckie Thistle!

The only good news is that the Incas will allow you to worship your old gods – as well as the new Incan ones.

Cheerless Chosen Women

Would you like to be an Incan 'Chosen Woman'? Sounds a bit special, doesn't it? If the Incas had advertised for Chosen Women they might have done it like this:

GIRLS!

THE CHANCE OF A LIFETIME!

Why don't **YOU** apply to be a

QUECHUA ACLLA CUNA

— that's right, a **CHOSEN WOMAN!**

GET TO LIVE IN THE TEMPLE!

NO MEN TO BOTHER YOU!

SIMPLE TASKS INCLUDE:
COOK THE HOLY FOOD. KEEP THE SACRED FIRE GOING.
WEAVE THE EMPEROR'S TEMPLE CLOTHES.

ALL YOU NEED IS TO BE BEAUTIFUL AND CLEVER
AND AGED BETWEEN 8 AND 10 YEARS!

STAY SHUT UP
FOR AT LEAST SIX
HAPPY YEARS!

THE LUCKY ONES
WILL LEAVE TO
MARRY LORDS! *

Apply to the matron (Mama Cuna) of your local temple or the
High Priestess (Coya Pasca) — the wife of the Sun god himself!

*The really lucky ones will end up as a temple sacrifice, of course.

By the 1500s there were several thousand of these Chosen
Women. Would you apply?

Apart from ending up as a temple sacrifice there was another danger in being a Chosen Woman ... You must never *ever* become pregnant. The punishment was pretty horrible...

Amazingly there *was* one way that a Chosen Woman could avoid this terrible treatment. All she had to do was say ...

... and she would be free!

Rotten royal roads

Another thing the Incas could do with conquered peoples was force them to work on building the Incan 'Royal Roads'.

Four roads led from the four quarters of the Incan kingdom and they met in the middle of Cuzco. The Incas called their empire 'Tahuantinsuyu' – which, as you know, means 'The Four Quarters of the World'. The four Royal Roads were important.

So what? you ask! So *you* try building a path down your back garden without…

- iron (for tools like shovels and pick–axes).
- written words (for making plans and organizing work).
- wheels (so everything had to be dragged).
- money (so paying workers and supplying them with food was tricky over big distances).

The Incas had none of these things!

The roads were useful for a fast messenger service across the empire and to move Incan armies quickly when trouble broke out. The Spanish conquistador Pedro de Cieza de Leon described one road…

> *In human memory no highway is as great as this. It is laid through deep valleys and over high mountains, through snow banks and swamps, through live rock and along raging rivers. In some places smooth and paved, in others tunnelled through cliffs, skirting gorges, linking snow peaks with stairways and rest stops, everywhere clean-swept and litter-free, with taverns, storehouses, and temples of the sun.*

The mountain roads had walls along the edge to stop you falling off the mountain. Very thoughtful, but a huge task to build hundreds of miles of walls. And doesn't it make you wonder who got the job of sweeping up the litter?

Marvellous messengers

The Incas had no way of writing things down (although they did have a clever recording system by tying knots in coloured string). Instead stories and messages were remembered.

There was no Postman Pat to carry letters around the Empire. Instead there was a relay-team of runners – the *chasqui*.

- These young men ran about a kilometre each to the next post and carried a message in their head. They then went back to their post and waited for the next message.

The chasqui chain were able to carry messages hundreds of miles across the Empire very quickly.

- The skill wasn't just in the running, but in the remembering. They had to get the messages exactly right, word for word. One word wrong and they would be punished – a bit like a history exam.
- The runners worked 15 days before they had some time off.

- They carried a badge to show they were servants of the emperor. They also carried a sling and a star-headed mace to defend themselves against wild animals.
- Messages were carried at around 150 miles a day – that's London to Cardiff if you want to look it up on a map.
- Messengers didn't just carry messages – they could be asked to carry food.

One emperor loved sea food and had it brought by messenger from the coast every day. If the fish wasn't fresh then the messenger was executed!

Did you know...?
The Incan armies marched north, south, east and west but they stopped at the edge of the Amazon rainforest. That rainforest was occupied by lowland tribes and many of them were head-hunters.

Wonder why they stopped there?

Horrible Huayna

Emperor Topa followed the trend of all the Incan emperors and died. (Around 1493 if you're interested in dates. Some people are, especially the sort you get in cakes.) He named son Huayna as next emperor … but then just before he died he said…

SORRY, CHAPS, I'VE CHANGED MY MIND. I NAME MY OTHER SON HUARI AS EMPEROR INSTEAD…

OVER YOUR DEAD BODY!

Huayna was a bit upset and his supporters murdered the guardian of young emperor Huari. Huayna got the throne he was supposed to have in the first place, so that was all right – unless you were Huari's guardian who got the chop, of course.

Remember, Incan emperors didn't get all their father's lands, which were shared out. A new emperor like Huayna had to go out and conquer more new land for himself. Huayna picked on the country we now call Ecuador, to the north.

He spent most of his reign battering Ecuador. In fact he liked it so much he thought he'd have a second capital city up there in Tumi Bamba. The lords back in Cuzco must have been shocked and horrified at the thought of a rival capital.

But before the Cuzco lords could revolt Huayna did a daft and deadly thing…

HUAYNA WAS IN ECUADOR WIPING OUT REBELS…

ME ARM'S GETTING TIRED!

SPLIP!

THEN A MESSAGE ARRIVED FROM CUZCO.

TELL ME YOUR MESSAGE WHILE I WIPE THESE LAST FEW REVOLTING PEOPLE OUT...

OH, DON'T MIND US...

DEAR EMPEROR HUAYNA,
HOPE THIS MESSAGE FINDS YOU WELL AND YOU ARE ENJOYING YOUR LITTLE BREAK UP THERE. I'M SURE YOU'RE DOING LOTS OF BLOOD-LETTING AND BUTCHERY TO KEEP THE PEASANTS IN THEIR PLACE.

ANYWAY, THINGS BACK HOME IN CUZCO ARE QUIET. VERY QUIET. NOW, DON'T GET TOO UPSET OR WORRIED, BUT THE REASON WHY THINGS ARE SO QUIET IS THE PEOPLE ARE DEAD OR DYING IN THEIR THOUSANDS. AND YOU DON'T GET MUCH QUIETER THAN A DEAD INCA.

IT SEEMS TO BE SOME SORT OF PLAGUE SWEEPING THE COUNTRY. IT'S COME FROM BOLIVIA. THE PEOPLE GO ALL FEVERISH AND SPOTTY AND DIE. LOTS OF THE WORKERS IN THE VALLEY ARE TURNING UP THEIR TOES AND HOPPING THE TWIG. IT'S JUST A MATTER OF TIME BEFORE THE PLAGUE REACHES

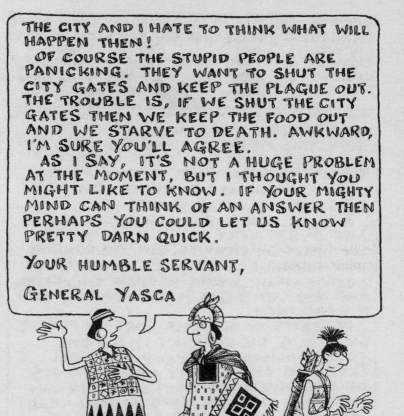

THE CITY AND I HATE TO THINK WHAT WILL HAPPEN THEN!

OF COURSE THE STUPID PEOPLE ARE PANICKING. THEY WANT TO SHUT THE CITY GATES AND KEEP THE PLAGUE OUT. THE TROUBLE IS, IF WE SHUT THE CITY GATES THEN WE KEEP THE FOOD OUT AND WE STARVE TO DEATH. AWKWARD, I'M SURE YOU'LL AGREE.

AS I SAY, IT'S NOT A HUGE PROBLEM AT THE MOMENT, BUT I THOUGHT YOU MIGHT LIKE TO KNOW. IF YOUR MIGHTY MIND CAN THINK OF AN ANSWER THEN PERHAPS YOU COULD LET US KNOW PRETTY DARN QUICK.

YOUR HUMBLE SERVANT,

GENERAL YASCA

Yes, it's tough at the top. You get the throne but you also get the problems. What could unhappy Huayna do? What would you do? Only an idiot Inca would rush back to Cuzco, catch the plague and die! But that's what Huayna did! He died so quickly he didn't name the next emperor … so that started another Incan punch-up for the throne. Nothing new there then.

Did you know…?

Huayna's son died a few days after his dad from the same plague. That meant two half-brothers (Huascar and Atahuallpa) were left to fight one another for the throne. While they were fighting, the Incan Empire was divided – just as Spanish invaders arrived. That's what made it so easy for the Spanish to defeat them.

You could say the Spanish plague was the first attack which helped the conquistadors to win. Maybe as many as eight million of the twelve million Incas died before the Spanish arrived. Invisible germs were the best weapons the Spanish could ever have had! Which just goes to show, 'Coughs and sneezes spread diseases … and spread Spanish empires with eases!'

Top of the class

Incan people were told what they should be doing at each age and what they should be wearing ... just like school. Only Incas never got to leave school the way you do.

Dire dress

Everyone had to wear what they were told. Each tribe had its own head-dress – and you were not allowed to pretend you were from another tribe by wearing their head-dress instead! You also had to dress the right way for your class – you couldn't be a peasant and dress too posh!

Peasant dress-sense

If you want to look like an Incan peasant here's how…

MEN

WOMEN

A LARGE CLOAK OVER THE SHOULDERS, TIED IN THE FRONT. (THE FINER THE CLOTH AND EMBROIDERY, THE HIGHER YOUR CLASS.)

A SLEEVELESS TUNIC

A BREECH-CLOTH

A SHOULDER MANTLE

A WRAPAROUND SKIRT THAT REACHED FROM BENEATH THE ARMS TO THE ANKLES, WITH THE TOP EDGES DRAWN OVER THE SHOULDERS AND FASTENED WITH STRAIGHT PINS.

A DECORATED SASH

Wee women

Girls! Now that you look like an Incan woman you need to dress your hair like the Incas. Here's how to do it…

1 Collect pee in a bucket. (Your family and friends can all chip in and help you fill that bucket fast.)

2 Leave the pee for a week to brew (the way beer is left to brew – except your pee won't end up tasting like brown ale).

3 Wash your hair by soaking it in the bucket of brewed pee. (This will get rid of the grease and leave your hair lovely and shiny – honest!)

4 When your hair is dry you can start making it into braids. To hold the hair in place wet it with some of that pee. (Hair spray hasn't been invented. Sorry.)

5 Find your Prince Charming and say…

Then hope that your Prince Charming likes a Cinderella who smells like a toilet!

Weather wizardry

The Incan family groups were called 'ayllu' and the head of a large family was called a 'curaca'. A curaca had power over everyone in the family … but you'd have to be crackers if you wanted to be one of the curacas. Curacas took the complaints from the family and went to the gods for help…

WE COULD DO WITH A BIT OF RAIN. HOW ABOUT IF I SACRIFICE THIS LLAMA TO YOU?

When it worked the curaca was a hero … but he also got the *blame* when things went wrong. What would you do if your garden was ruined by a drought?

A Spaniard described what happened to one clumsy curaca…

A powerful curaca called Fempellec was the ruler of his village. This lord moved the statue of a god from the temple. The villagers said that this made the gods angry and they sent a terrible drought. His people died. The priests then took Fempellec and drowned him.

If there was a drought then how could they drown him? The Spaniard didn't explain. Maybe they drowned him in a dried-up river?

Would you kill your dad for a dried-up garden? (On second thoughts you'd better not answer that!)

Mister masters

Men ruled Tahuantinsuyu. Women worked and had children but had no power. A man, though, could increase his power by having children. It was almost like a supermarket loyalty card – the more points you had the richer you were … except instead of points you had children and wives.

THE TUZCO BONUS OFFER

MEN! TAKE THE INCA TRAIL TO POWER!
It's so simple!
JUST COLLECT THOSE KIDS AND WIN
TERRIFIC TITLES
5 CUTE KIDS AND YOU'LL BE NAMED
'LITTLE OVERSEER'
FOR JUST 10 CHARMING CHILDREN
WE'LL NAME YOU 'OVERSEER'
BUT GO FOR THE JACKPOT!

A MAN WITH A FABULOUS FAMILY OF 50
CAN BE LORD OF HIS OWN VILLAGE!

Yes! You too can be a cool Curaca. Start right now collecting the wonderful wives that will take you to the Tuzco Top!

Remember our motto:
THE MORE THE MERRIER!

More children meant more workers to produce more food and more power … for the men.

Keeping in class

Now you are ready to live like an Inca. What you *did* each day depended on your age. The Incan laws told you exactly what you should be doing. They divided their people into 12 classes. If the Incas could have written their rules down they'd probably have looked something like this…

1 **Babies** (in arms) and 2 **Infants** (up to one year): In the care of their parents.

3 **Children** (aged 1–9): Children aged 1–5 may play. Children aged 5–9 must help parents in small tasks. Girls must help mind the babies, cart water and animal feed, weed, and help the women make beer. At age 5 girls must start to learn how

to weave. Girls planning to be servants will be sent away to be trained.

4 **Youths** (aged 9–16): Boys to be trained as *llamamechecs* (llama herders of the llama herds). Girls aged 9–12 will gather flowers and herbs for the dyeing of textiles and for medicinal use. Girls aged 12–16 will work at home, keeping house and

producing textiles (though some may serve as *llamamechecs*). Girls are allowed to marry at 14, although most will wait until they are 18.

5 Young men (aged 16–20) and **6 Prime men** (aged 20–25): Will work as post-runners, as senior llama herdsmen to the *llamamechecs*, and as servants to military officers.

7 Young women (aged 18–30): Women are considered full adults at 18 (unlike men who will not become adults until 25.) At this age they should be wives and mothers.

8 Puric (men 25–50): This age group of men should be married. At 25, they will be heads of households. They must learn to farm their given piece of land and pay taxes and serve in the army if they are called to. They might also be sent out to some remote part of the empire to pioneer it and to keep an eye on any hostile or disloyal natives in the area. Some men in this class are also called on to work in the state's mines.

9 Unmarried women and widows (women 30–50): They will make pottery and cloth, and work as house servants.

10 Old men (aged 50–60): These men are semi-retired and have no state or army duties. They are expected to help out from time to time during harvest and planting seasons, or to do light work as public officers, clerks, and storekeepers.

11 Elders (aged 60–80): Both men and women will eat, sleep, and may do light work if they are up to it, such as tending guinea pigs. They are pensioners and are tended to by the state.

12 Invalids (sick and disabled): They are expected to work as their disabilities allow, but are otherwise in the care of the state.

You'll notice there is no class at all for people over 80, so it seems not too many Incas made it that long! Imagine having your whole life planned for you by the government like this! Still, there was always death to look forward to.

Stinging school

You will also notice there's no school in there for you peasants. But if you were a lord's child then you would get four years of lessons…

INCAN SCHOOL TIMETABLE
YEAR 1: THE INCAN LANGUAGE (QUECHUA)
YEAR 2: RELIGION
YEAR 3: KNOTTED STRING (QUIPUS)
YEAR 4: HISTORY

Imagine! A whole year doing history! Horrible!

Of course you could make it more fun by messing about in lessons, but be warned! The punishment was pretty nasty…

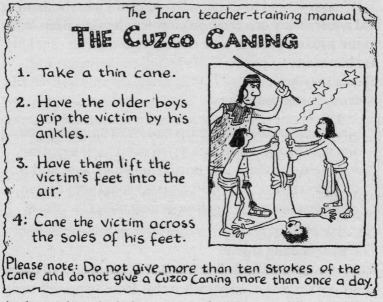

The Incan teacher-training manual

THE CUZCO CANING

1. Take a thin cane.

2. Have the older boys grip the victim by his ankles.

3. Have them lift the victim's feet into the air.

4. Cane the victim across the soles of his feet.

Please note: Do not give more than ten strokes of the cane and do not give a Cuzco Caning more than once a day.

And you thought being sent to do sums outside your head-teacher's door was nasty!

Shake, rattle and stroll

Of course the festivals would give you a few days off school. There would be a parade of men playing drums, tambourines, flutes and pototoes ... no, not *potatoes*, dummy! The pototo was a large shell (called a conch) that was blown like a trumpet.

ONE POTOTO, TWO POTOTO, THREE POTOTO, FOUR...

When you went to the parade you could join the dancing and wear 'shaker bracelets' on your wrists and ankles. What would you use to make your rattling bracelets?

a) glass beads
b) small seashells
c) dried llamas' toenails

Answer: **c)** Dried llamas' toenails, of course. Pop along to your local llama sacrifice with a pair of pliers and rip the toenails out before the rest of the animal is burned as a sacrifice. Dry them in the sun, drill a hole in each one and thread them on to a string. You're ready to rattle!

The pulverizing Puric

You can see from the Incan class list that the men who went off to serve in the emperor's army were expected to be married at that age. This meant that the men had to leave their wives behind.

An old Incan legend, passed on by word of mouth, tells of the dramatic result of this on one family...

Once upon a time there was a young man, a Puric, who was sent for to serve as a soldier. He had to leave his young son and his wife.

'I will miss you both,' he sniffed.

'I'll miss you too,' his wife snivelled.

'And I'll mith you motht of all!' the little boy lithpt ... I mean *lisped*.

When the Puric had left, his wife wept over her weaving and cried over her cooking and sobbed over her sewing. 'Don't cwy, Mummy!' the little boy said.

Suddenly a breeze blew a white butterfly through the window. 'It's a signal from my husband,' the woman whispered. 'So long as the butterfly visits I will know he is safe!'

'What dat?' her son said and pointed a podgy finger at the butterfly.

His mother sighed, 'It's my lover!'

And so they lived happily till the Puric returned. As it happened the little boy was pulling weeds in the garden so he was the first to see his father marching down the road. He ran on to the road and the Puric swept the boy up into his strong arms. 'My son! How have you been?'

'Gweat!' the little boy laughed.

The man stopped and put him down. 'Weren't you upset? Weren't you and Mummy lonely?' he gasped.

'No!' the little boy laughed. 'Mummy's lover came to thee her everwee day!'

The man picked up his mighty club, raced into the house and smashed his wife till she was a crushed corpse.

The little boy came in and saw the butterfly flutter round the head of his panting father. 'Look, Daddy!' he cried. 'Here is Mummy's lover, come to thee her!'

Live like a lord

It seems to have been much more fun to be an Incan emperor. Why not try it and find out what it was like? If you want to be Incan emperor (Sapa Inca) of your class then here's a quick guide...

You looking at me, mate?

The Sapa Inca is descended from the sun – a sort of sun son. No one can look at the sun, so no one can look at *you* directly. Wherever you go your subjects must look down ... or else. When the lower classes want to speak to you they must turn their backs and bow to show respect. (Though someone turning and bowing may show their backside, which hardly shows respect!) At court the Sapa Inca often sat behind a screen.

Make your own screen

① Take one old door.
② Nail planks to base.
③ Attach label.

DON'T LOOK AT ME OR YOU'LL GO BLIND. TURN YOUR BACK AND BOW

Atahuallpa spoke from behind a screen to his brother who passed on the messages like a walking cordless telephone.

Tassel hassle

It's no use being an emperor if you don't let people know you're in charge. As Sapa Inca you wear a special fringe *not* a crown. On your head-dress you wear a fringe of red, woollen tassels hung from little gold tubes.

How to make a Sapa Inca head-dress

① Cut straws in half and paint them gold.
② Thread through red wool to leave tassels at one end.
③ Stick the tasseled tubes to a headband.

GOLD

Tinge that fringe

Pick your heir – the favourite son of yours who will take the throne when you die or decide to retire. Your heir wears his hair under a fringe that's tinged bright yellow. (Try saying that with a mouthful of mushy peas!) He also has a stick with a feather on it that sticks out 10 cm from his forehead.

51

Plug that lug

Pierce your ears. Male members of the Incan royal family and nobles of pure Incan blood wore huge earplugs (earrings that stretch pierced ears). Unlike anyone else in the empire they cropped their hair. The size of hole in your ear shows how noble you are; the larger the hole, the more noble the wearer. A conquistador said…

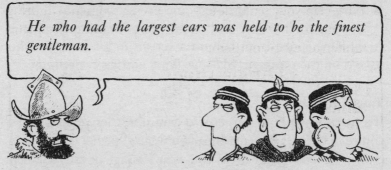

He who had the largest ears was held to be the finest gentleman.

Francisco Pizarro, the Spaniard who came and conquered the Incas, was amazed to see that the Incan king had earlobes that hung to his shoulders and that the ear discs worn by some Incan nobles were as large as oranges. You could try this short cut to emperer-sized ear-lobes…

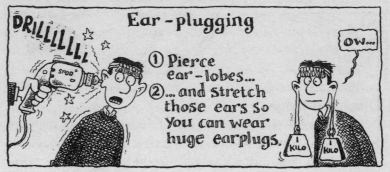

Ear-plugging

DRILLLLLLL

① Pierce ear-lobes…
② …and stretch those ears so you can wear huge earplugs.

OW…

1 KILO   1 KILO

Perhaps the strangest custom of all was for the royal family to fit earplugs … to their llamas!

Nibble your nosh

The Incas didn't have tables. They ate off cloths on the floor. But you are an emperor! We can't have that.

- First, sit on your throne – a curved piece of wood about 20 cm high.
- Send everyone else out of the room – because a Sapa Inca always eats alone.
- Now clap your hands and your serving women will bring in your food – they will stand there, holding the plates while you eat from them.

Throne alone

(School dinner ladies)

But there is one Sapa Inca habit you probably shouldn't try at home – or in your school dinner hall. A conquistador said …

If the emperor coughed or spat, a woman held out her hand and he spat into her palm. And any hairs that fell from his head on to his clothes were picked up by the women and eaten. The reason for these customs is known; the spitting was a royal thing to do; the hairs because he was afraid of being bewitched.

Yeuch!

Pick up that litter

As Sapa Inca you are too grand to walk. You will be carried everywhere in a 'litter'.

Lounging litter

① Nail your chair to two poles.

② Cover the chair with a box.

air-holes

The holes in the side let the air in and let the emperor see out, but peasants can't see in. Why not train 20 strong and steady litter-carriers and go for a quick run down the motorway? Your wives and your treasure can follow on in hammock–litters.

Live like an Inca

Crime time

There was very little crime in Tahuantinsuyu because everyone shared what they owned so there was no point in stealing. But what would happen to a man who murdered his wife? Well, for a start, he would NOT be locked in prison.

There were three main crimes to be punished: murder, insulting the emperor, and insulting the gods. The punishment for these was death and the Incas had a nice simple way to execute someone. What was it?

a) They would cut the criminal to pieces and feed them to the guinea pigs.
b) They would drown the criminal in Lake Titicaca.
c) They would throw the criminal off a cliff.

Answer: c) Which would you prefer?

A rare, but really serious crime was to have one of the emperor's wives as a girlfriend. The punishment was to be stripped naked, tied to a wall and left to starve to death.

Smaller crimes had lesser punishments – nice little things like having hands or feet chopped off or eyes gouged out! (The criminal could see the point of the punishment ... but then not much else!)

Particular punishments

We have 'set' punishments for some crimes today. So a motorist who drives 10 miles an hour above the speed limit will be fined a set amount and have 'penalty points' put on his or her driving licence. The Incas didn't have money so they didn't have fines and they didn't have driving licences … possibly because they had no paper. But they did have 'set' punishments for certain crimes.

Could you be a law enforcer in Tahuantinsuyu? Match the crime to the powerful punishment …

FOR THE CRIME OF...

1. BEING A WITCH OR WIZARD
2. KILLING AN ASSISTANT (IF YOU'RE A GOVERNMENT WORKER)
3. REBELLION AGAINST THE STATE
4. GOING AGAINST THE LAWS OF THE GODS
5. TREASON AGAINST THE EMPEROR

THE PUNISHMENT WAS TO BE...

a) GIVEN A SLOW AND AGONIZING DEATH AND THEIR BONES TURNED INTO MUSICAL INSTRUMENTS — TOOT!

b) BEATEN TO DEATH AND THE BODY LEFT TO BE EATEN BY GIANT BIRDS CALLED CONDORS

c) BURNED ALIVE, HAVING HIS HOUSE BURNED TO THE GROUND, THE TREES UPROOTED AND THE CROPS DESTROYED

d) PLACED IN A CAVE FULL OF DANGEROUS ANIMALS FOR TWO DAYS — GRR! OOOER!

e) LAID FACE DOWN ON THE GROUND AND A STONE DROPPED FROM A METRE HIGH ONTO THE BACK

In the cave of Sancay, prisoners convicted of treason were placed in a cavern full of wild animals, toxic toads, and venomous reptiles. If a convict survived two days in these surroundings he was pardoned and released, since his survival seemed to signal that he was obviously under the protection of the gods.

Answers: **1b)** … witch is not very pleasant.

2e) This sometimes killed the prisoner. If it didn't then he was left with severe injuries for the rest of his life.

3a) It's nice to think that, after you are dead, your bones will give people so much pleasure, isn't it?

4c) Seems a bit cruel to punish the trees! Maybe they just picked ash trees to match the ash owner!

5d) A conquistador described this punishment…

Foul food

Beastly beer

When the Incas had a festival they enjoyed large amounts of their 'chicha' beer. It's probably more fun to watch llamas being slaughtered when you've had a few pints!

Do you have a school assembly you have to go to? Need a cup or two of chicha to give you strength? Then follow these simple (but disgusting) Incan instructions…

On the other hand you may prefer to stick to lemonade – without the spit.

Tasty tatties

The Incas ate lots of potatoes. One of their words for these vegetables was 'papa' which Spanish invaders changed a little to give us the modern word 'potato'. But the Incas and the tribes they conquered had over 200 other words for potatoes! (I wonder who counted them?)

We only have about a dozen …

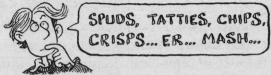

SPUDS, TATTIES, CHIPS, CRISPS... ER... MASH...

The Incas even had dried potatoes long before they appeared in your local supermarket. They picked their potatoes in the autumn when the Andes days were warm and the nights fell below freezing. Then they'd…

- spread the potatoes on the ground overnight to freeze
- let them thaw the next morning
- gather them into large piles in the afternoon
- trample them under their bare feet to squeeze out the water
- spread out the pulp to dry
- store it over the winter months
- add water whenever they fancied some spuds – just like today's packets of dried potato.

The potato crop, like the rest of the Incan farm food, was divided into three equal parts…

- one for the village
- one for the stores in case of famine
- one for the priests to burn as a gift to the gods.

Wood was scarce in some parts of the Andes so how did you roast your potatoes? Over a fire of dried llama droppings, of course! (Well, you enjoy Smoky Bacon crisps – why not Roast Llama Dropping flavour?)

SCRUNCH SCRUNCH SCRUNCH YECH!

ACTUALLY THE LLAMA DROPPINGS TASTE BETTER!

Terrible treatments

The Incas were fairly healthy with no plague-type diseases – until the conquistadors brought them as a special gift from Spain! But they did have some sicknesses … and some ways to treat them that your local doctor would probably not advise today…

Cuzco Cures

Reliable remedies for ill Incas

Wicked wounds: Got a nasty llama bite? Been stabbed or stoned by an enemy warrior? Simply take the bark from a pepper tree, boil it in water and slap it on the wound. It's hot stuff for curing wounds is the pepper tree.

Dreadful diarrhoea: Take the leaves from the coca plant and chew them. These wonderful leaves also help lessen your hunger and stop you feeling sick when you climb those high mountains.

Awful aches: Take a glass knife and gouge a hole between your eyes. This will cure your headache in no time! Or if the pain is in your arm then let out arm blood – you'll see that there's no 'arm in it!

Hot tots: If baby has a fever then collect the family pee in a pot and wash baby in the lovely liquid. If that doesn't work then give it to baby to drink! Yummy drink from Mummy!

Ill infants: All sensible mothers cut their baby's umbilical cord when it's born then dry it and store it. When the child falls sick just give it the umbilical cord to suck on and it will suck the pain and evil spirits from its body!

Horrible headaches: Draw an oval on the skull then drill holes along it about a quarter centimetre each. Lift out the bone and let out the evil spirits from the head. Another way is to saw two lines at right angles. Of course the patient would like plenty of coca leaves to drug them while you do this! There's nothing like a hole in the head to drain the pain!

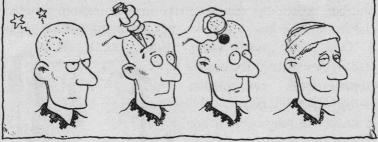

It seems that the hole-in-the-head treatment worked. Archaeologists have found skulls with these pieces removed and it is clear the wound healed and the patient survived.

Village healers also used a special trick to make sick people believe they were cured. First they fed the patient black and white corn flour then hypnotized them into a trance. While the family watched, the healer pretended to open up the

patient's stomach with a knife. He would then appear to pull out a nasty collection of snakes, toads and other objects. (Naturally this was a conjuring trick.) They then cleaned the blood off the body and said, 'Look! The wound is healed and all this poison inside you is gone!'

The patient would feel better because they really *believed* they'd been cured.

Brush up your appearance

Boys! There's nothing a girl hates more than rotten teeth and bad breath. So why not make sure your teeth are clean the Incan way? Here's how …

1 Take some molle twigs (from the South American pepper tree – the garden hedge will NOT do).

2 Roast the twigs over a hot fire till the ends are smoking.

3 Place the hot roast twig against your gums.

A conquistador described what happened next…

The twigs scald the gums, the burnt flesh falls off to reveal new flesh underneath. This new flesh is very red and healthy!

Now, lads, go out and find your dream girl. With luck she will be a cannibal who enjoys kissing a lad who tastes of roasted human flesh.

HORRIBLE HISTORIES HEALTH WARNING
Do not try this! A baboon's bum is red and healthy but you wouldn't want it in your mouth! Remember, smoking can damage your health … and so can putting a smoking twig into your mouth.

Funny money

The Incas didn't use money. They exchanged their work for what they wanted. Good idea for school…

CLEAN THE BLACKBOARD AND YOU GET A BAR OF CHOCOLATE!

WHAT DO I GET IF I CLEAN THE TOILET?

SMELLY HANDS

They also used materials and clothing as a sort of money. Not such a good idea…

It isn't as if a sort of money hadn't been invented. The Sican people (conquered by the Incas) used copper axe-heads as coins. You can make these yourself and be the richest Sican in your class. All you need is half a tonne of sheets of copper and a big hammer. Cut and hammer the copper into axe-head shapes. Each one is about 5 cm long by 3 cm wide.

Rich Sican lords were buried with up to 500 kg of these axe-heads, stacked up in piles of 500 around them. Sican lords were also buried with up to twenty human sacrifices.

The Incas never copied the idea of copper-axe money, which may not be a bad thing. After all, the Bible says the love of money is the root of all evil. So maybe the Incas simply decided the copper axe-coins were just axing for trouble!

Funnier money

Another reason the Incas had no money may be to do with the way they *thought*. So, you and your parents and the people in your country *think*…

A RICH PERSON IS SOMEONE WITH A LOT OF MONEY…

… but an Inca would think…

A RICH PERSON IS SOMEONE WITH LOTS OF FOLLOWERS…

The conquistadors never really understood this. An Incan lord would have lots of wives so he could have lots of children and grandchildren – that would make him 'rich'. The Spanish were horrified and wanted to hang an Incan lord, Don Juan, because he had lots of wives.

Don Juan tried to save his life in two ways…

1 Don Juan gave a fortune in buried treasure to the Spanish officer who wanted him executed. It was valuable to the Spaniard, but not to Don Juan.

65

2 The Spanish officer said, 'Send your extra wives to the home of a good Christian woman to learn Christianity.' Don Juan sent the Incan women ... but cheated and kept his favourite extra wife at home. He sent another woman in her place.

Sadly the Spanish discovered the bribery and the trickery. Don Juan was very quickly hanged ... for doing what his ancestors had always done.

Inca Inquisition

Have you noticed how teachers like to ask you questions? Why do they bother when they probably know the answers?

It's time to turn the tables and torment your teacher with this simple quiz. If they get less than 5 out of 10 they are probably ready for early retirement. If they get more than 5 out of 10 then they were probably around in Incan times and are ready for retirement anyway! Answer true or false...

1 When an Inca became too old to work they were turned into a mummy and buried ... even if they weren't dead!

THIS IS NO WAY TO TREAT YOUR MUMMY!

2 Old people were given the job of collecting lice.
3 Inca Huaca was released by the people who captured him because he cried.
4 Atahuallpa's leading general, Chalcuchinma, had his legs burned to a crisp to get him to reveal Incan treasure stores.

5 Emperor Atahuallpa's chair carriers gave up when the Spanish chopped off their hands.

6 Modern Peruvian men have mock sling fights in memory of their Incan ancestors, but no one gets hurt.

7 The Incan warriors were expert archers.

8 The Incas enjoyed popcorn.

9 The Incas ate dogs.

10 The Incas rode on llamas.

Answers:

1 False. The Incas were among the first people to look after their old people. They had the first old age pensions – food supplies not money, of course. Some of the emperor's wealth was set aside for widows, orphans, old people and the disabled. The emperor's collectors took more food and materials than they needed, then they stored it in case there was a drought or a famine. (A bit like the way you save in a piggy bank. But, being from the Andes they probably had guinea-piggy banks!) The blind were given the task of picking seeds out of cotton plants and were paid with food and shelter.

2 True. When you were too old to farm you went to the Incan food store and you collected your old-age food pension. This was usually at the age of fifty. (Nowadays you get a bus pass at sixty and that's all – and they taste terrible.) But the old were expected to make themselves useful. Collecting firewood ... and collecting lice. You then took your collection of lice to the leader of your family group.

LICE TO MEET YOU.

3 True. But Huaca had an incredible talent ... he cried tears of blood! His captors were so amazed they set him free. (Don't try it yourself or you'll make a right mess of this book.)

4 True. But don't feel too sorry for the general. His favourite sport was drinking from the skulls of dead enemies. He survived the charred legs to go on and poison the emperor who took Atahuallpa's place. Not a nice man.

GRRR!

5 False. It is TRUE that they had their hands chopped off … but they did NOT give up their work, carrying Atahuallpa around the country! They carried the covered chair (litter) on their shoulders until they bled to death. (Maybe they carried on because they were devoted servants – or maybe because the Incas had a law against dropping their litter!)

6 False. The men from rival regions fight one another like knights fighting for the love of beautiful girls. These are mock fights yet every year several men get themselves killed.

7 False. The warriors preferred to use stones fired from slings. They didn't use bows and arrows because good wood for bows doesn't grow in the Andes.

8 True. Corn was their main food and they ate it toasted, boiled or ground into flour and baked. They also heated it till it 'popped'. Pity they didn't invent the cinema to go with the popcorn.

9 False. The Incas conquered the Huanca tribe and the Huanca loved to eat dog as a special treat. The Incas were a bit disgusted by this. They much preferred to eat guinea pigs (roasted or in a stew). The little furry friends ran around the house like pets till they were wanted for dinner. The Incas also ate llama meat (tastes a bit like mutton) but generally not much meat at all.

10 False. Llamas were used like donkeys to carry loads but the Incas never rode them. Probably because the llamas have a nasty habit of stopping and sitting down for hours on end if they are overloaded or upset! The Incas were also wary of the llamas' greatest skill – spitting a long way, with a great aim, at anything (or anyone).

The cruel conquest

By 1532 the Incas had conquered dozens of states and ruled over 12 million people who spoke at least 20 different languages. Their empire stretched 2,000 miles from north to south and 500 miles east to west.

But the Spanish had discovered America thanks to Christopher Columbus. They smashed the Aztecs in Central America then they began to march south, looking for treasure. The Incas were attacked by Spanish invaders – all 250 of them! (Oh, all right, 198 soldiers and 62 horsemen if you want to be picky.)

So the Incas outnumbered the Spanish about 60,000 to 1. No contest?

Timeline

1526 Francisco Pizarro from Spain lands on the coast of Peru and is welcomed by the rich Incas. He is given lots of gold – he'll be back for more, of course. Next time he'll have an army!

1527 Emperor Huascar, one of Huayna's sons, takes the throne. His half-brother, Lord Atahuallpa, decides to fight him for it. Atahuallpa wins and captures Huascar.

1532 Pizarro and his little army arrive back in Peru and meet the young emperor Atahuallpa. The Spanish kidnap Atahuallpa and hold him to ransom. Many Incas believe

the Spanish could be fair-skinned gods. They don't fight.

1533 The Incas pay Atahuallpa's ransom, but the Spanish execute him anyway. That is a very sneaky thing to do. End of Incan Empire and the start of Peru's suffering.

1537 Incan rebel Manco Capac II sets up a new Incan kingdom at Vilcabamba. It can't last.

1541 Pizarro is assassinated … not by the Incas though. This is a seriously unpopular bloke.

1572 The last Incan rebel stronghold is captured and emperor Tupac Amaru, son of Manco, is beheaded. Without a head the new Incan Empire is finished – and without a head Tupac Amaru isn't too grand either!

1600 For every hundred Incas alive when the Spanish arrived there are now only ten. Slavery and diseases from Europe have almost wiped them out in seventy years.

1782 Tupac Amaru II, descendant of last Incan emperor, leads a revolution against Spanish rule … and fails. The Spanish make him watch the executions of his wife and sons, then they hang, draw and quarter him. (And you thought the Incas were cruel?)

1808 South American countries begin to rebel against Spanish rule. **1824** The Spanish are defeated and new countries are formed. In the old Incan homeland the country of Peru is set up.

Peculiar Peru

The Incas said they lived in Tahuantinsuyu. So, how come the Spanish arrived and called it Peru? Here's how…

The Spanish landed on the east coast of America. In 1511 the Spanish conquistador, Balboa, was weighing some gold when a young Amerindian chieftain struck the scales with his fist and said…

Then the Spanish heard stories of 'The Golden Man' – a South American king who was so wealthy he covered himself in gold dust every morning before he took a bath in his holy lake.

The Incas were doomed from that moment. It took the Spanish twenty years to find 'Peru'. But once conquistador Pizarro arrived the Incas had had their chips. (Pizza and chips have always gone well together.)

Powerful Pizarro

The leading conquistador in Tahuantinsuyu was the Spaniard Francisco Pizarro (or Franny to you and me). With his 260 men he conquered millions of Incas. Who was this Pizarro? Some sort of Superman? Here are some terrible truths…

Franny's fantastic facts

1 Franny grew up in Spain as a poor boy whose job was to look after the pigs. That's where he first learned to bring home the bacon.

2 It is said that his parents ran away and left him. He survived because he was brought up by a sow!

3 Franny never learned how to write (the sow never taught him). He couldn't even write his own name and it was needed on the official documents. So what did Franny do? He had a stencil made of his name and coloured it in when he needed to sign a paper!

4 Franny joined the explorer Nunez de Balboa when he crossed Panama and discovered the Pacific Ocean in 1513. Balboa was beheaded by the king's trusted general, Pedrarias Davila. Franny wasn't daft and he became a follower of Davila and kept his head.

5 Franny then joined up with the soldier Diego de Almagro and they set off to conquer lands south of Panama. The people of Panama couldn't believe anyone could take such a risk – they nicknamed Almagro and Pizarro's little army 'the band of lunatics'. The Panama people were right; Franny came back with just a little gold – and left behind a lot of dead soldiers.

6 On his next expedition into South America Franny was wounded by arrows seven times but carried on.

Franny and 250 Spanish soldiers retreated to the safety of an island where he made a famous speech. He drew a line in the sand and said …

> *Gentlemen, this line is work, hunger, thirst, weariness and sickness. If you wish to join me in facing these perils then cross the line and stand beside me like true friends. No matter how few there are, I know that we will be victorious.*

Would you cross the line? How many of those 250 gallant Spanish men crossed Franny's line? Was it …
a) 13?
b) 113?
c) 213?

Answer: **a)** Just 13 swallowed this brave talk and joined him. He must have felt a bit of a twit!

7 Like all great leaders Franny had a lot of luck. One of his 'Glorious Thirteen' was a giant of a man called Pedro de Candia. This man offered to explore the trail ahead alone. He said …

> *If I'm killed you will only have lost one man which is not important. But if I succeed your glory will be great!*

De Candia carried a metre-long wooden cross and marched towards the Incan town of Tumbez. It's said the Tumbez councillors released the Emperor's lion and tiger on to the path. The creatures weren't hungry and lay down at de Candia's feet. He patted them on the head and the people of Tumbez were gobsmacked. Or god-smacked. They were sure de Candia had come from the sun god and worshipped him.

HE'S CONQUISTADORABLE!

8 Peru was peppered with Pizarros. Franny's three brothers helped him to conquer the country. None of the brothers lived happily ever after. One, Hernando, went back to Spain and was locked in prison for 20 years for his great work! He was released and died at the age of 100 in terrible poverty.

Plotting Pizarro

The Spanish arrived in Tahuantinsuyu looking for gold. The King of Spain had given them ships and paid the Spanish soldiers. In return he wanted South American gold. Lots of it. Lots and lots and lots of it.

Exam time for teacher. Ask your history teacher, 'Can you answer each of these questions in just two words…?' (Of course they'll fail! Teachers can never use two words when two hundred will do!)

Franny Pizarro may not have been able to read and write … but at least he could answer these horrible historical challenges. Could you?

Question 1: How did a handful of Spanish conquistadors defeat the vast numbers of Incan warriors?

Answer: They cheated.

Pizarro led his men into the city of Cajamarca – the Incas thought this might have been a visit from some wandering gods and didn't try to resist.

Then Pizarro sent a message to Emperor Atahuallpa…

Pizarro then had his cannon hidden covering the square and horsemen in the side streets. The Incas had never seen a cannon or a horse before. When Atahuallpa's bodyguard marched into the square the cannon opened fire and the horsemen rode in to finish them off. Up to seven thousand were butchered and Atahuallpa was taken prisoner. It makes those Spanish soldiers sound like brave but heartless killers. Yet Pedro Pizarro, who was there, said …

While they waited for the signal many Spaniards wet their pants from terror without noticing it.

Pizarro may sound like a ruthless and cruel villain. But then Atahuallpa's plan had been to capture the Spanish, sacrifice some of them to the gods and turn the others to slaves ... after cutting off their naughty bits. Pizarro just got his attack in first!

Question 2: How did Pizarro get the Incan wealth from all corners of the 2,000 mile empire?

EASY PEASY!

Answer: Ransom Atahuallpa.

That way you get the Incan people to bring their treasure to you! Pizarro had Emperor Atahuallpa locked in a cell. He simply said …

IF YOU WANT YOUR EMPEROR BACK, THEN I WANT THE CELL FILLED WITH GOLD!

The Incas, incredibly, agreed. They brought 13,265 pounds of gold (6,017 kilos, give or take a nugget). They also brought 26 pounds (12 kilos) of silver. I guess that was their small change. It took the Incas eight months to bring all the treasure to the city.

Question 3: How did Pizarro make sure Atahuallpa didn't destroy him once the ransom was paid?

HMM...

Answer: Kill Atahuallpa.

Oh, yes, I know the Incas imagined their Emperor would be set free once the ransom was paid. But Pizarro wasn't daft. He never planned to let Atahuallpa go.

He said to Atahuallpa, 'We will burn you to death!'

That upset the Emperor a bit because he wanted his body to be turned into a mummy after death … and it's a bit hard to make anything out of ashes (unless it's an ashtray, of course).

Pizarro made a deal. 'Tell you what, Atty, old man. If you agree to become a Christian then I'll be really kind to you and have you strangled instead!'

Atahuallpa agreed.

The Emperor was tied to a stake, a cord was placed round his throat and tightened by twisting a stick until he was strangled – a cheerful little execution method called the garrotte.

IT'S NO CHOKING MATTER!

Of course Atahuallpa didn't mind too much ... he was sure he'd be reborn again! Emperors didn't die, they just found a new body!

The Incan armies were lost without their leader and the small group of conquistadors easily took control. Pizarro had just one problem ... and it wasn't with the Incas...

Awful Almagro

The trouble with being a great success is that some people will get jealous and hate you. If you want to be popular then be a failure and everyone will love you! The man who hated Franny Pizarro more than anyone was fellow Spanish conquistador, Diego de Almagro.

- Almagro and Pizarro conquered Tahuantinsuyu between them but Pizarro was the Spanish King's pet and Almagro got jealous.
- Almagro was sent south to help conquer Chile. Not only did he fail, but the Incas in Cuzco rebelled while he was away.
- When Almagro returned to fight the rebels he turned to Pizarro's brothers for help ... but they refused to obey his orders during the fighting.
- Almagro put the brothers in prison and Pizarro was not a happy bunny.

- Spaniard fought Spaniard as Pizarro attacked Almagro. When Pizarro captured his old friend he showed Almagro the same mercy he'd shown to Atahuallpa. He had him strangled in the same way – then had his head cut off just to make sure!

YOU CAN'T BE TOO CAREFUL!

Getting it In-ca neck

Almagro's expedition to Chile was a disaster because he made some daft mistakes. For a start he set off over the mountains in winter. Even the tough Incan helpers froze to death. Almagro set out with 12,000 Incas and 10,000 died in that first winter.

The Incas were chained together in long lines with iron collars around their necks ...

When an Inca fell sick it would take a long time, with frozen fingers and cold keys, to unfasten that collar. Almagro came up with a quick way of removing the Inca from the neck collar so the march wasn't held up for long. What was Almagro's short cut?

Answer: He chopped off the Inca's head.

Did you know…?

Almagro wasn't the only conquistador to fail in Chile. The next conquistador to return to Chile, Pedro de Valdivia, who tried to take over the region in the 1550s, died when the Indians poured molten gold down his throat, saying,

> *You came for gold, now we give you all the gold you can use.*

Franny's finale

Franny was killed by Almagro's son and his Spanish friends in the end, not by the Incas. He had built himself a palace in Lima and that's where they got him. But he went down fighting. He killed two of his attackers and then they came up with a wonderful plan – they threw one of their mates at Pizarro's sword! (Nice friendly thing to do!) As Pizarro tried to pull his sword out of this third corpse they stabbed him in the throat.

Franny died a Christian. He dipped a finger in the blood from his throat and made the sign of a cross on the floor. He kissed the bloody cross … then the last blows rained down on him. Plenty of people went to the funeral but no one cried. The leader of the assassins, Almagro's son, got the chop a year later.

Awesome Atahuallpa

It's easy to say, 'Aw! Poor Atahuallpa! Tricked and murdered. It's not fair!' But the truth is Atahuallpa took the throne from his half-brother with trickery and murder ... so perhaps he got what he deserved!

Atahuallpa ruled in the north – Atahuallpa had been his dad's favourite so Dad gave him a region of his own before he died. But that made the new Emperor (Atahuallpa's brother Huascar) nervous. First Atahuallpa promised to obey the Emperor...

He sent the best soldiers he had, armed to the teeth! By the time Huascar realized this was actually an invading army it was too late. He was captured and his guards slaughtered in front of his eyes.

Atahuallpa wasn't finished ...

When they arrived he had them all put to death! That left the main danger lying in Atahuallpa's royal family – his 200 or so brothers and cousins.

> I WANT THEM SACRIFICED! I WANT THEM HANGED, OR THROWN INTO A LAKE WITH STONES AROUND THEIR NECKS, OR THROWN FROM A CLIFF... AND YOU CAN LET HUASCAR WATCH THE FUN!

That should do it, eh? No. The women and children of the royal family had to go next. They were starved and then hung by the neck or the waist and left to die. (A Spanish writer said they were hung 'in ways too disgusting to mention' ... so we won't mention them.)

Enough, Atahuallpa? Nope! The servants and water-carriers and gardeners and cooks were massacred too. In some cities just one man remained for every ten women.

Now he was safe from his half-brother. The trouble was he had weakened his fighting men when the threat came from the Spanish invaders.

Awfully big mistake, Atahuallpa!

The men with soft swords
Atahuallpa had defeated Huascar when he heard about the strangers who had arrived. He also heard about their guns, swords and horses – the things that would defeat him.

But the Incan generals didn't want to scare Atahuallpa so they told him a few little fibs…

> THEY HAVE THESE THINGS CALLED 'GUNS' – BUT THEY CAN ONLY STRIKE TWICE AND THEN THEY'RE FINISHED!

> THEY HAVE THESE STICKS CALLED 'SWORDS' – BUT THEY ARE AS SOFT AND HARMLESS AS A WOMAN'S WEAVING STICK!

> THEY HAVE THESE CREATURES CALLED 'HORSES' – BUT THEY ARE POWERLESS TO MOVE AT NIGHT!

> NOTHING TO FEAR THEN, CHAPS! LET'S MEET THEM AT SUNSET AND WE'LL BE FINE!

They did … and they weren't! When Atahuallpa arrived a priest explained the Christian religion to the Emperor … in Latin! He handed Atahuallpa a Bible … but the Emperor didn't even know what a book was! Not surprisingly, Atahuallpa was bored with the sermon and threw the Bible down. That was when the hidden conquistadors struck. A Spaniard wrote …

> *It was a wonderful thing to see. To see so great a lord as Atahuallpa, who came with such power, taken prisoner in so short a time.*

The writer also enjoyed the fact that while thousands of Incas were killed, not one conquistador died.

While Atahuallpa was imprisoned he didn't forget his brother Huascar. He sent out secret orders to have Huascar killed!

Silvery suffering

The Incan peasants had worked for their leaders and in return their leaders had cared for them. But the Spanish conquistadors made the Incan peasants work with just enough to keep them alive.

The greatest suffering was in the silver mines. The Spanish back in Spain were desperate for money (to pay soldiers to fight wars). The silver mine at Potosi was discovered and the Spanish worked the Incas to death to get its treasures.

Yet it wasn't the Spanish who discovered the mine. It was a llama herder. The story goes like this ...

The shaking mountain was probably a small earthquake.

That old story of angry gods didn't bother the Spanish when they heard it. In 1571 they started mining for the silver and paid the workers with what?

a) pieces of the silver
b) pieces of farmland
c) pieces of cloth

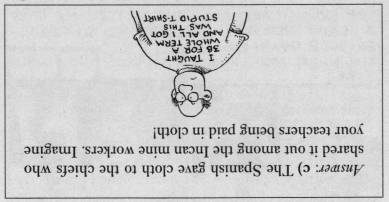

Answer: **c)** The Spanish gave cloth to the chiefs who shared it out among the Incan mine workers. Imagine your teachers being paid in cloth!

So many Incas suffered in those mines they must have wished that herder had kept his mouth shut.

Working woes

The Spanish found new ways to make money from the Incas and brought them new ways to die...

- In the silver mines the workers would sweat to fill their cloaks with rocks then drag them to the surface. When they reached the cold air at the top of the mine they were chilled and many caught pneumonia and died.
- In the mercury mines the mercury could be breathed in with the dust and could poison the miners. It gave them raw throats, fever and a slow death.
- In the sugar-cane factories the Spanish brought in heavy machines to crush the sugar cane. They often ended up with crushed Incan peasants as well.

Routed rebels

Of course the Incas tried to rebel against Spanish rule from time to time. Not very successfully. They not only failed but suffered terribly.

During Manco Capac's Easter Uprising, in 1536, Spanish soldiers came towards the city to put down the uprising, and the Incan fighters taunted the Europeans by lifting their bare legs at them! (The insult is still used in the Andes.) Insulting, perhaps – but not very effective!

THIS'LL SHOW 'EM!

The battle raged for over a month. The Spanish tried terror tactics: they chopped up Indian women and cut off the right hands of captive warriors to toss them out of their fortress for the Indians to find.

After the Cuzco uprising, Pizarro first tried to befriend Manco Capac. That failed, so the Conquistador had Manco's sister-wife...

- stripped
- tied to a tree
- whipped with rods
- shot to death with arrows.

Then her corpse was put in a basket and floated downstream into the Incan camp.

Pizarro also burned alive Manco's best general and 15 other important Incan captains.

Manco thought he'd made friends with a Spanish ally of Almagro, but the Spaniard stabbed him to death. Some friend.

Terrific temples

When the conquistadors arrived in Cuzco they could scarcely believe their eyes. In fact conquistador Pedro de Cieza de Leon said ...

> *If I wrote down everything I saw then no one would believe me!*

But in his book *Chronicle of Peru* he wrote down enough to give a glittering glimpse into the strange world where they came, they saw and they robbed.

> *We reached their Coricancha, the Incan House of the Sun. Around the wall, half-way up, was a band of gold, two palms wide and four fingers thick. The many doorways and the doors were covered in gold and inside the walls were four houses. The houses were not very large but each was covered with plates of gold on the outside and the inside.*

No wonder the greedy Spanish eyes popped out!

But the Incas didn't just cover their Sun Temple with gold. They were also great artists and filled the palace with golden models. Imagine Madame Tussaud's where everything is made of gold instead of wax!

In one of the temple houses was the figure of the sun, large and made of gold. It was cleverly made and studded with precious stones.

They also had a garden, but the soil was made from golden nuggets, and solid golden corn grew there. There were twenty llamas with their lambs, shepherds guarding them with slings and crooks – every single thing made of gold.

There were huge numbers of jars and pots and vases, all made of gold or silver and studded with emeralds.

And, in the Incan world every scrap of gold belonged to just one man: the Emperor. The Spanish planned to change that completely … and for ever. They stripped off the gold, melted down the statues and shipped the lot back to Spain!

Savage sacrifices

What did the Incas actually *do* in thei̶... made sacrifices to their sun god. If you ca̶... plated palace, 100 metres long and 30 metres wide, ... can try this for yourself...

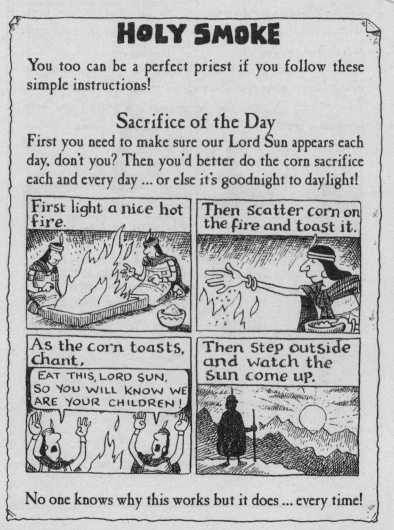

HOLY SMOKE

You too can be a perfect priest if you follow these simple instructions!

Sacrifice of the Day

First you need to make sure our Lord Sun appears each day, don't you? Then you'd better do the corn sacrifice each and every day ... or else it's goodnight to daylight!

First light a nice hot fire.

Then scatter corn on the fire and toast it.

As the corn toasts, chant,

EAT THIS, LORD SUN, SO YOU WILL KNOW WE ARE YOUR CHILDREN!

Then step outside and watch the sun come up.

No one knows why this works but it does ... every time!

Sacrifice of the Month

On the first day of each month, take a hundred pure white llamas.

Lead your llamas round to the images of the gods.

Divide the llamas among the thirty priests of the temple (one priest for each day of the month).

Massacre the llamas, throw chunks of their flesh on to the fire, then grind their bones into powder for use in your services.

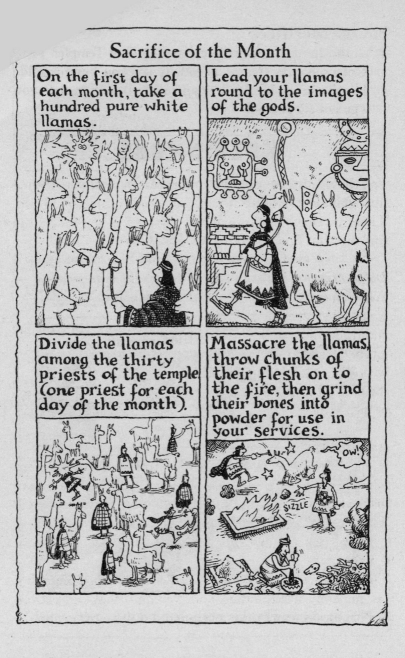

Yes, those cute little bundles of fur, guinea pigs, were turned into guinea pork as sacrifices. But don't cringe too much. There are worse things than roasting pets, as you're about to find out. But first ...

Did you know ...?
When an emperor died the Incas would often pluck out *his eyebrows* and throw them to the wind as a gift to the gods. Goodness knows what the gods would do with them! Maybe make eyebrow wigs of their own?

OH GREAT. MORE EYE-BROWS. JUST WHAT I NEEDED...

Killing kids

If the Incas were in desperate trouble – defeat in battle, famine or plague – only *human* blood was good enough to bribe the gods. And the purest blood was a child's blood. The Incas believed their gods preferred a nice sweet kid!

Cold graves

The Incas made their human sacrifices up in the mountains. Germs don't like the thin mountain air – they can't afford oxygen masks – and the constant cold is like a fridge. So the child sacrifices haven't rotted away. They are still there to be found after 500 years.

A newspaper report in April 1999 described one find, an Incan sacrifice in Argentina …

She was found 22,000 feet up on the summit of the Lullaillaco volcano in the north-west Argentine Andes. The 500-year-old girl's face looks peaceful in spite of the way she died. They got her drunk on beer and she was numb with the cold before she was wrapped in blankets and brightly coloured cloth. Then she was buried alive.

The little Incan girl's face is the best preserved of any ever found. She and another boy and girl were naturally mummified by the extreme cold and lack of oxygen.

Scans have shown that their organs are not damaged, there appears to be frozen blood in their veins and the remains of their last meals are still in their bowels. The girl, whose face can be seen poking through the dusty rags, was about 14. Her cheeks are swollen but she looks like one of the dark-skinned children who play in the streets of Salta today, in the shadow of the mountain their ancestors worshipped.

Happy gods mean sunny days

It sounds incredibly cruel to take a child to the top of a mountain then bury them alive. But the Incas believed they were doing the right thing. If you asked an Incan priest they would have given you reasons …

WHY PICK ON INNOCENT CHILDREN?

BECAUSE THEY ARE INNOCENT. THAT'S WHAT THE GODS PREFER.

WHY KILL ANYONE AT ALL?

IT IS A PAYMENT TO THE MOUNTAIN GOD. HE BRINGS US THE SUN AND THE RAIN. WE SEND THE CHILDREN AS MESSENGERS TO SAY THANKS.

DON'T THE PARENTS MIND?

NO, IT'S A GREAT HONOUR TO HAVE YOUR CHILD SACRIFICED. SOME CHILDREN ARE CHOSEN YEARS IN ADVANCE. THEY ARE SPECIALLY FED ON SACRED CORN.

ISN'T IT HORRIBLY CRUEL?

NO! WE DON'T RIP OUT LIVING HEARTS THE WAY THE AZTECS IN MEXICO DO. WE SEND THE CHILDREN TO SLEEP QUIETLY.

So children went to a gruesome death to keep a god happy. Very often the sacrifices were made as a way of saying 'Thank you!' to a god for a great victory in battle.

Terror for teenies

The journey to the top of the mountain took days, with stops every night in bare stone shelters.

Did the children know that death was waiting for them at the top of that mountain? In spite of the beer they had to dope them, the children must have been terrified.

An archaeologist described one find …

> The crown of the boy's skull is as bare as an eggshell. His adult teeth are just coming through. There is a crack caused by a heavy blow that killed him. Through the crack you can see his shrunken brain. But he still has a face and it looks twisted with what looks like fear.

Was it fear? Or was that just the imagination of the archaeologist?

Grave robbers

The child sacrifices were buried with a small supply of food, so they'd have something to eat on the journey to the next world. They were also buried with sea shells and gold figures of men, women and llamas.

The Spanish conquered Tahuantinsuyu in order to steal Incan gold, and treasure-hunters *still* wreck old graves to steal the golden images. They don't care about the history they are destroying and they certainly don't have any respect for the poor dead children. An archaeologist came across one grave that had been blown apart with dynamite…

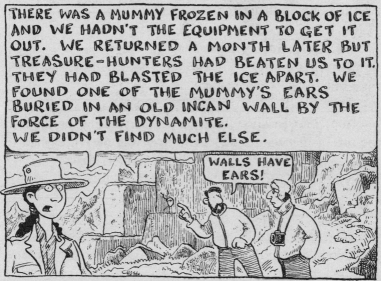

THERE WAS A MUMMY FROZEN IN A BLOCK OF ICE AND WE HADN'T THE EQUIPMENT TO GET IT OUT. WE RETURNED A MONTH LATER BUT TREASURE-HUNTERS HAD BEATEN US TO IT. THEY HAD BLASTED THE ICE APART. WE FOUND ONE OF THE MUMMY'S EARS BURIED IN AN OLD INCAN WALL BY THE FORCE OF THE DYNAMITE. WE DIDN'T FIND MUCH ELSE.

WALLS HAVE EARS!

The statues are often sold to rich collectors so they can't be seen in museums where the rest of us can study them. It isn't only the Incas and the conquistadors who are ruthless, greedy and selfish.

Pointy heads

Some of the child victims have been found with strange-shaped heads. It seems that they had wood strapped to their heads from the moment they were born so the infant heads were forced to grow to a point. The head took on the shape of the mountain on which they'd be sacrificed!

What if the mountain had twin peaks? Then the Incan parents managed to bind the children's heads in such a way that the skull grew into two peaks! Horrible but true!

And, after all that effort, they killed them.

Modern mummy murders

Archaeologists who visit the sites to examine sacrificed mummies make a gruesome claim ...

SOME PEOPLE STILL MAKE SACRIFICES TO THE MOUNTAIN GODS TO THIS DAY... PEOPLE ARE IN JAIL TO PROVE IT. THERE HAVE BEEN ARRESTS!

Another visitor to the Incan lands that are now in Argentina said ...

COUNTRY PEOPLE STILL CLIMB THE MOUNTAINS TO LEAVE GIFTS OF GRAIN. ONE OLD MAN SWORE THAT LOCAL SUGAR PLANTATION BOSSES KILL AND EAT ONE OF THEIR WORKERS EVERY YEAR TO MAKE SURE THEY HAVE A GOOD CROP.

Which is a bit like a head-teacher killing and eating a pupil every year to make sure they have good exam results! Let's hope no head-teacher reads this book.

Did you know…?
You may think the Incas were bloodthirsty, but some of the other tribes in Tahuantinsuyu were worse. The Spanish Friar Valverde, who baptized Atahuallpa, tried to flee when Francisco Pizarro was assassinated. He got to Ecuador, but was captured by Indians in Puná, who killed him … then ate him. (They probably sold him at a Friar Tuck shop.)

Llucky llama

In April each year the Incas had a ceremony in honour of Napa – the white llama. A white llama was dressed in a red shirt and had gold ear ornaments attached. He drank chicha beer and chewed coca leaves, the same as the priests.

Then he made a chicha sacrifice to the gods. How on earth can a llama make a sacrifice? Pots of chicha were laid out in the temple and the llama was sent in to kick them over! (Bet you wouldn't have thought of that!) And the biggest treat for the llama wasn't the beer … it was the fact that the priests let him live. The Napa llama was never sacrificed!

Other llamas weren't so lucky…

- two 'red' llamas were always sacrificed at a wedding
- 100 llamas were sacrificed every month at the Sun Temple
- thousands of llamas were sacrificed to the gods before a big battle

What if there were a drought or a famine? What would the people do?

That's an awful llot of llama.

And you really wouldn't want to know how the priests went about sacrificing a llama, would you? You would? Oh, very well, they slit their throats. (And that makes a right mess on a white llama's coat.)

And you really wouldn't want to know what the priests did with the blood, would you? You would? You *are* sick! If you must know the priest drank some of the blood and scattered the rest on the ground.

Did you know…?

Modern visitors to the ancient sacrifice site at Mount Sara Sara can stock up with food for the journey. In the villages at the foot of the mountain you can buy dried frogs. This is to make that popular dish, frog soup. If that's what you enjoy then hop over to Peru!

Groovy gods

Who were these gods who had to be kept supplied with fresh meat? The Incan gods could be grim and gruesome – like a lot of gods in a lot of countries. Here are a few for you to worship if you feel like it.

Viracocha

Job: Creator of Earth, humans and animals.

You may like to use one of his other names...

- Lord Instructor of the World (Sounds like he was a head-teacher!)
- The Ancient One (Yes ... definitely a head-teacher!)
- The Old Man of the Sky.

Tall tales: Viracocha not only made humans – he also destroyed them, made them again out of stone, then scattered them around the world. After teaching humans how to survive he took his cloak, made it into a boat and sailed off into the Pacific Ocean.

Some Incas said that was a silly story ...

HE DID **NOT** MAKE HIS CLOAK INTO A BOAT! THE TRUTH IS, HE WALKED ON THE WATER!

OH YEAH, MUCH MORE LIKELY!

Viracocha was a good friend to the Incas. When Emperor Pachacuti was under attack by the Chanca, Viracocha appeared to him in a dream and encouraged the Emperor on to victory. Pachacuti made a temple to Viracocha in Cuzco to say 'Thanks'. Appearance: Pachacuti had the god's image made in gold. This figure was about the size of a 10-year-old child. Was Viracocha a small god? Or was Pachacuti just a bit mean with the gold?

Inti

Job: Sun god.

He is named after an Incan emperor called Inti, which means 'My Father', because Inti was thought to be the parent of the Incan lords.

Appearance: A human face on a golden disc with sun-rays around the edge.

Mama-Kilya

Job: Moon mother and wife of Inti

Tall tales: The Incas believed that when Mama Moon cried her tears fell as silver. (A very handy mama to have if you need some extra pocket money! Chop an onion under her nose and get enough to buy a new computer game!)

Apu Illapu

Job: Rain-giver and god of thunder.

This was the god the common people prayed to mostly because rain was so important to them.

Terrible tales: Temples to Apu were usually in high places. When the people needed rain they climbed up to the temple and made a sacrifice. This was often a human sacrifice. It was a sort of straight swap – a human life for a shower of rain.

(If your grandad's cabbage patch needs some rain then you may like to sacrifice a history teacher to Apu and see if it works.)

Appearance: You can't see Apu but you can see his shadow – it's the band of stars we call the Milky Way. The Incas believed Apu took his water from the Milky Way. (That's daft, of course, because it would rain Milky Rain if it was true. The streets would be covered in butter!)

Pray-time

The Incas had priests and temples in every corner of their empire and a chief priest in Cuzco who was nearly as powerful as the Emperor.

As well as a temple you could pray at a 'huaca' – that's a holy place. But this holy place could be…

- a mountain
- a bridge
- a mummy (especially the mummy of a dead emperor)
- a cairn (a pile of stones by the side of a road – add a stone and the gods will grant you a safe journey).

Mummy magic

Going into battle? Then you need the help of the dead Incan emperors. Here's how to get it …

1 Take out their mummies and parade them in front of the warriors. (There was no mummy of the first emperor, Manco Capac, who turned to stone when he died.)

2 Get a military band to play music on bone flutes (made from human shin-bones) and tambourines.

3 Have poets recite long epic poems about the dead emperors. You may want to try this when your school next does battle with a rival school in soccer, hockey, netball or tiddlywinks. Parade your mummies while the school orchestra plays and recite an Incan epic. If you don't know any Incan epics then make one up, something like this …

HERE'S OUR MUMMY, SINCHI ROCA,
TRY TO STOP US AND WE'LL CHOKE YER!
AND THE MUMMY OF OUR LLOQUE,
WE CAN'T LOSE WITH THIS GREAT BLOKE!
MAYTA IS THE NEXT IN LINE,
WE WILL BEAT YOU EVERY TIME.
FOLLOWED BY THE GREAT YUPANQUI,
WE WILL STOP YOUR HANKY PANKY!
INCA ROCA IS THE NEXT,
WHEN WE BEAT YOU, YOU'LL BE VEXED!
SEE THE FAMOUS LORD HUACAC,
HE'LL BE WITH US IN ATTACK!
VIRACOCHA, MIGHTY LORD,
HE'LL CHEER WHEN WE'VE SCORED!

Scary! No wonder the Incas won most of their battles!

Make that mummy

The emperor mummies were different to the sacrifice mummies that are found frozen on the mountain tops today. The emperor mummies were prepared more like Egyptian mummies. Their insides were taken out and they were stuffed with herbs. The eyes were then taken out (nice job for someone) and replaced with shells that were made to look like eyes.

The emperor's mummy was then stored carefully and well looked after by a team of servants. They made sure their mummy-monarch had...

• regular changes of clothes
• a cloth laid with his favourite food each day
• a special treat ... visits from the most beautiful of the Chosen Women from the temple.

It was never boring being an emperor's mummy. As well as getting out and about in parades he would also be visited by the royal family who wanted advice. All in all it was a hectic and tiring life being dead.

Horrible horoscopes

The Incas believed that life was controlled by the gods and you had to check with them before you did anything. With the help of the priests you could...

- discover a criminal
- tell who would win a battle
- find the cure for a sickness.

The best place to chat to a god was at an 'oracle', a place where the god would make himself known. The oracle at the Huaca-chaca bridge must have looked a bit weird. A conquistador described it like this ...

The Incas spoke to the oracle and the spirit of the river spoke back to them. (A pole as thick as a fat man could have

held a priest as fat as a thin man inside, couldn't it? The priest could answer the question – then get to eat the sacrifice when the Incas had gone.) This may sound very artistic and charming. It wasn't. Spanish visitors reported that these 'oracles' were spattered with blood from sacrifices – often human blood.

Here are some other ways to find out about the future...

Faking firemen

It wasn't just priests at oracles who could cheat. There were men called *yacarca* who would speak to the spirits in a fire and answer your questions. They blew through a tube to make the fire glow red hot. The fire spirits then 'spoke' to anyone who wanted an answer to a question. But a clever-clogs conquistador spotted that the *yacarca* was actually a 'ventriloquist' – speaking the fire-spirit answers without moving his lips!

Coca crawlers

Another way to tell the future was to look at a dish of leaves picked from the coca plant. (A bit like reading the future by looking at tea leaves in a cup as some people still do today.) You could also take a powerful drugged drink called *ayahuasca* and see the future in the wild dreams it gave you. But strangest of all was to watch the way a spider wandered across the floor. That would tell you everything you wanted to know!

Llama lungs

Watching spiders not strange enough for you? Then try this …

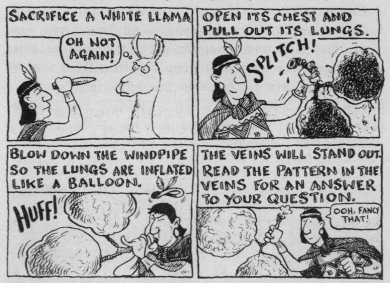

Remember, it must be a *white llama*. Next-door's cat is just not good enough.

Strange signs

An ancient Incan story said that one day strangers would land in Peru and destroy both the Incas and their religion. Emperor Huayna was worried, but especially when in 1532 he received more 'signs' from the gods…

- At the Feast of the Sun an eagle appeared, chased by a flock of buzzards, and fell at the Emperor's feet. The priests fed and cared for it but the eagle died. What was the meaning? If the king of birds could be destroyed then so could an emperor?
- There were an unusual number of earthquakes. Great rocks shattered, mountains crumbled and tidal waves

swamped the shores. What was the meaning? If a mountain could fall then so could an emperor?

- Comets filled the sky and the moon appeared to have three rings of light around it – one blood-red, one greenish-black and one smoky-grey. Of course the moon was believed to be the Emperor's mother. What was the meaning? A priest explained to the Emperor ...

THE BLOOD-RED RING AROUND YOUR 'MOTHER' MEANS THAT WHEN YOU DIE A CRUEL WAR WILL BREAK OUT AMONGST YOUR PEOPLE. BLOOD WILL BE SHED IN STREAMS. THE BLACK RING MEANS THAT NOTHING WILL SURVIVE OF OUR RELIGION. EVERYTHING WILL VANISH IN SMOKE – THAT IS THE THIRD RING!

Three years later Huayna died, the Spanish had arrived with a new religion and the priest's words came true. Amazing! (Bet you wish that predicting-priest was around today. He could tell you next Saturday's lottery numbers!)

So how did the Incas think they might avoid their dreadful fate? By keeping the gods happy with lots of sacrifices: when Huayna died the Incas killed four *thousand* people to be buried with him. (And a fat lot of good it did them.) All because of a dead bird, a few earthquakes and a ring round the moon.

Fossil fuel

Who was the most important member of an Incan family? Dad? No. Mum? No. Mummy? Yes!

The ancient founder of a family – like your great-great … grandad – would have been turned into a mummy and was the family's most valuable member. In fact if another family kidnapped your mummy it could be held to ransom!

The Spanish arrived and were shocked at the way the Incas worshipped their ancestors. What did the conquistadors do with the mummies?

a) gave them a Christian burial

b) burned them

c) turned the mummies into shop–window dummies

Answer: **b)** Don't try this with your grandad … especially if he's not dead yet.

Good God

Once the Incan emperors had been defeated the Incas squabbled among themselves. Some rebelled and some made friends with the Spanish invaders. Inca killed Inca and Spaniard killed Spaniard as they fought over land and gold and religion.

The Spanish tried to make the Incas worship the Christian God, rather than Incan gods and mummies. But just when the plan seemed to be working a Spanish priest made a horrifying discovery. He told the governor the shocking news. His letter may have read something like this …

Parinacochas Village
Peru
21 June 1564

Your Grace,

The whole of Peru is in terrible danger. I discovered the truth here in my own parish. Send help at once. Send soldiers. Send arms.

I had noticed that the Indian men in my village disappeared every night to a large meeting hut. They wouldn't let me in! Me! Their priest! But I waited till they were all inside and listened at the door.

First they began to pray, and I realized they were praying to their old Incan gods. If that wasn't bad enough, one of their leaders (Curacas as they called them) stood up and began to scream at them. I remember his evil words now.

'The Christians have one God, they say. But we Incas have many more powerful ones. We also have hundreds and thousands of ancestors who care

PTO ⟶

113

for us. They have told us that the Incan gods are going to rise up and destroy the Christian God! Floods will be sent to wash away all traces of the Spanish. We can start again. The Spanish will die. So will any Incas who follow them. If we Incas want to survive we must stop worshipping the Christian God and we must stop obeying the Spanish. Our gods are hungry and thirsty because Incas have stopped giving them Chicha beer and sacrifices. We must start again!'

The Incas say their gods are coming down from the hills and taking over their bodies. Some of these 'possessed' people shake, tremble and fall, or dance insanely.

After their meeting I took one of the weaker villagers and said I would burn him if he didn't tell me everything. It seems this rebel movement is spreading across Peru. We must destroy their holy places and burn their mummies. If we don't we will all die. In God's name, send help! Send help!

Your devoted servant,
Father Luis de Olivera

The Spanish sent investigators and discovered the rebellion was spreading fast. It took them three years to destroy all the holy places (huacas) they could find. They also destroyed 8,000 Incan rebels. The rebellion failed. Their mummies had let them down!

Purify that priest
The Incas found it painful to rebel against the Spanish Christians. Rebel Incas went on doing it in secret. These Incas thought Spanish priests made the Tahuantinsuyu ground impure by walking on it. So, after the priests had gone, they used a horribly historical way of cleaning their pathways...

Don't try this at home! Dead dogs in rivers can pollute the water, kill the fish and make drinking water dreadful.

A 1613 revolt against the Catholic Church was crushed by the Spanish and the leaders arrested. These Incan leaders were so upset they poisoned themselves rather than become Christians.

And when one Incan leader (a Curaca) failed to support his people they poisoned him. But that sort of violence was rare. Most Incas pretended to be Christians but went on worshipping the Incan gods too.

Terrible tales

Do you have a really grotty little brother or sister? Offer to read them a little good-night story ... then tell them this terrifying tale from Peru. The Spanish brought their superstitions as well as their religion to Peru, including a dreadful fear of cats who were thought to be mixed up in witchcraft and black magic.

Are you comfortable, dear little brother (or sister)? Then I'll begin.

 Once upon a time in Peru there was a six-year-old boy called Jose. Now, Jose had a cruel and wicked grandfather called Manuel. The grandfather drank lots of strong wine at the local tavern but that didn't make him happy! No, it put him into a terrible temper and he could be really nasty. (He also had very smelly feet, but that's not important so I won't mention it.)

One night Grandfather Manuel staggered back from the local tavern in a terrible rage.

'I'm in a terrible rage!' he roared.

'W-w-w-why?' Jose asked.

Grandfather Manuel frowned and his ugly face twisted in disgust. It was as if someone had stuck his smelly feet under his nose. 'Don't ask stupid questions!' he roared. 'Ooooh! Me chest!' he gasped.

The old man's eyes popped, his knees flopped, his tongue swelled, his feet smelled and he fell forward, flat on his ugly face, dead!

'Ooooh! What a shame!' the people of the village wailed on the streets.

'Yippee!' the people of the village cheered when they were alone in their homes.

That was until they heard about the strange will he had written before he died. Grandmother Consuela read it to little Jose (who was a bit too young to read).

I, Manuel, order that the following must be done when I die:

1. My funeral to be held at midnight.
2. My coffin to be left open.
3. There must be enough chairs for all the people who will want to come.
4. My body must not be taken to church and there must be no priest at the funeral.

Grandmother Consuela quivered and Jose shivered. 'I can smell the fires of Hell in this!' the old woman wailed.

'I thought it was the smell of his feet,' her grandson sighed.

The evil smell filled the room where the coffin lay. No one came to visit the corpse – who can blame them?

At midnight a distant church bell rang. In the trembling silence a black cat stalked into the room. It had eyes as red as the coals of Hell. It was followed by a second cat, then a third and more. Soon every chair in the room was filled by a black cat with red eyes.

Grandmother Consuela whispered, 'Black cats are sent by the devil himself!'

'Why?' Jose asked.

'To claim the soul of the dead!' she croaked.

'His sole? The soles of his feet? Is that why they smell so bad?' the boy asked.

Before she could reply a cat started to wail and soon every cat in the room joined in to make a fearful noise like a school violin lesson.

The candles flickered and there was a soft creaking of the coffin. Grandfather Manuel sat up. His eyes were lifeless as ever but his body moved. First one smelly foot, then the other, was swung over the side of the coffin and the corpse stood on stiff legs.

The black cats marched from the room, tails held high, and the corpse shuffled out behind them.

'Where's Grandfather Manuel going?' little Jose asked.

Grandmother Consuela chewed her knuckles and mumbled. (You'd mumble too if you had a mouthful of knuckle.) 'He was an evil man in life, now his punishment is to have no peace in death. The devil has made Grandfather a *condenando* ... he must wander the earth for ever more, never sleep and never rest!'

'Ooooh! That's horrible,' Jose sighed.

Grandmother Consuela jabbed a bony finger at the boy. 'And that's what'll happen to you if you are wicked or cruel to your big brother (or sister)! The black cats will come to get you!'

When you've finished the story your really grotty little brother or sister will have learned an important lesson from Spanish Peru. If they ever dare to upset you again all you have to say (as they say to nasty nippers in Peru to this day) is, 'Is that a black cat I see over there?'

Inca mystery quiz

An Inca would look at you and think, 'Goodness me! These 21st century people are strange! They kill one another with metal machines called "cars"! Children play games with moving pictures where they learn to massacre hundreds of people on machines called "computers"! They have delicious meat but mash it up and fry it till it tastes like a dung-beetle's birthday cake and they call it a "burger"!'

There's nothing odd about Incan life – it's just that it looks that way to you. So here is a perfectly sensible Inca quiz...

1 The Incan people liked to keep their dead kings happy. How?
a) They fed them lots of beer so they could be Incan drinkas.
b) They put the latest books in the grave so they could be Incan thinkas.
c) They changed the shoes on the kingly corpses every week because they didn't want them to be Incan stinkas.

2 We call everyone who lived in the Empire 'Incas' today. But in those days 'Inca' was a word that was used for what?
a) Only the men (because women didn't matter)?
b) Only the people of Cuzco (because conquered people didn't matter).
c) Only the royal family (because no one else mattered).

3 The Incan Empire of Pachacuti stretched from the Amazon rainforest in the east almost to the Pacific Coast in the west. Why did the Incas not settle on the west coast?

a) Because it was too wet.

b) Because it was too dry.

c) Because they were afraid that sea monsters would jump out and eat them.

4 An Incan emperor wore a 'poncho' coat just once. What happened to each of these ponchos once he'd finished with it for the day?

a) They were given to the poor to keep them warm.

b) They were sacrificed to the gods.

c) They were stored in a special poncho palace.

5 Cuzco, like much of the Incan homelands, was 4,000 metres above sea level where the air is thin and most humans would struggle to breathe. How did the Incas manage?

a) They had really big strong hearts for pumping what little oxygen there was around their bodies.

b) They had big noses and big mouths so they could gulp down more air than most people.

c) They had big air tanks like aqualungs (made from llama skin) that they filled each day with lowland air and carried home to breathe.

6 How did the Incan men get rid of their facial hair?

a) They smothered their whiskers in honey and put their face in an anthill. The ants chewed off the honey and the hair. (That's a sweet idea.)

b) They shaved using razors made from sharp sea shells. (Shore is a good idea.)

c) They pulled their whiskers out one at a time using bronze tweezers. (They needed to be pretty plucky!)

7 When an Inca killed an enemy what could he use the dead man's skin for?

a) To cover a drum ... so the enemy will be beaten twice! (Boom! Boom!)

b) To wrap some sandwiches for the journey home.

c) To scrape thin enough to let light through and use as a window in the family home.

8 An Incan princess died accidentally on a hunting trip. Her heartbroken Incan love, Illi Yunqui, buried his dead princess in the Lake of the Incas, high in the Andes. It is said that the water changed colour as her corpse splashed in and it's still that colour today. What colour?

a) Red, from her blood.

b) Green, the colour of her eyes.

c) Gold, the colour of the jewellery buried with her.

9 What nickname did the Spanish conquistadors give to the Incas when they first met them?
a) Big Ears.
b) Noddies.
c) Mr Plods.

10 A conquistador rode up to Emperor Atahuallpa and stopped just short of trampling him – it was meant to show how powerful the Spanish were. Atahuallpa didn't so much as blink ... but some of his warriors did. How did Atahuallpa reward the warriors who had shown so much fear for their Emperor?
a) He gave them each their weight in gold for being so loyal.
b) He gave them a painful death for being cowards.
c) He gave them a llama to practise trick–riding like the Spanish.

Answers:
1a) The Incan lords made some peasants produce extra grain to brew into beer. This beer was then 'fed' to the mummies of the dead kings who probably became dead drunk as a result.

2c) Only the royal family were 'Incas' in Incan times. The Lord of Cuzco himself had the title 'Sapa' Inca – meaning 'King'. There were never more than 1,800 pure-blood Incas of the royal family. But, when they ran short of a royal to rule they could 'adopt' a trusted outsider. These 'adopted' Incan royals were called 'Hahua' Incas.

3b) The shoreline of the Pacific was dry and not suitable for growing crops. It's said that anyone living there might see a shower of rain once or twice *in their lifetime!* The Incas probably could have conquered it if they'd really wanted.

4b) The poncho was taken to a temple where it was burned as a sacrifice to the gods. You may like to try this with your dad's smelly socks.

5a) Incan hearts could carry 60% more blood round the body than the average human. And blood carries oxygen to the brain and the muscles that need it. The air was thin but the Incan people got more of it. (And put on a dunce's cap and go to the bottom of the class if you answered **c**).) The Incas also seemed to survive the cold better. A Spanish monk, Barnabe Cobos said …

I'm amazed at how warm the Incas are in the coldest weather, and how they can sleep on snow a palm's width deep. They lie on it as if it was a feather bed. I believe the reason is they have stomachs as tough as an ostrich's!

Uh?

6c) Incan men plucked their facial hair out with bronze tweezers. These tweezers were so valuable to them they were buried with their owners. That's a good idea and it must work because you never see an Incan mummy with a beard!

7a) The Incas went into battle playing drums and tambourines made with the skin of dead enemies.

8b) The lake is green, said to be the colour of her eyes. (No one has trawled the lake for her corpse to find out if she really did have green eyes. Anyway the fish have probably scoffed them.) It is said that on still winter nights you can still hear the moans of her heartbroken love. (More likely to be some tourist moaning, 'My God, it's cold up here! I wish I'd worn me thermal knickers!')

9a) They called them Big Ears because of the way the Incas stretched their ear lobes to wear big ornaments.

10b) An example of how Atahuallpa's soldiers were treated very strictly. They always did what they were told. So, when Atahuallpa told them not to harm the conquistadors they didn't. They didn't fight back when the conquistadors began to massacre them! Atahuallpa's ruthless rule backfired on him.

Epilogue

No one says the Incan emperors were kind rulers. But the Incan people suffered far, far more under the Spanish conquistadors.

The Incan way of life had some good ideas. They said that everyone should help everyone else with everything. The government tried to make sure that this happened. Life would be so much easier if that happened today!

The Incas also had some pretty dodgy ideas. They believed in Heaven and Hell like their Spanish conquerors, but they were a little different. Heaven was the sun where the good people went for warmth and food – Hell was inside the Earth where the bad suffered cold and hunger. So children, who were too young to be evil, would go to Heaven and happiness ... and by burying a child sacrifice alive you were doing the child a favour!

But they lived in a harsh world where earthquakes and landslides could destroy all they'd spent years building, where it could take days to walk just a few miles and where survival depended on the warmth and the kindness of the sun. It was a brutal world so it's not surprising there could be brutal people in it.

Pachacuti was one of the greatest ever native Americans. As he lay dying he managed to be quite poetic about his fate ...

Like a lily in the garden I was born,
Like a lily I grew up.
Years passed, I grew old.
I withered and died.

He could have been writing about the tribes who inhabited the Andes before the Incas. He could have been writing about the Incan nation itself. He could have been writing about the conquistadors.

All a bunch of lilies.

A bitter Incan survivor of the conquest wrote a poem to his gods about the fate of the Incas ...

You are lying spirits,
You are cruel and devilish enemies.
You are the cause of my misery and my failure!
I have adored you with all my power,
I have worshipped you with great sacrifices,
With human sacrifices.
You are just greedy robbers
And cruel enemies of my soldiers.
You shall be cursed for what you have done.
None of my children will worship you,
Not even the tiniest girl-child,
And not my royal grandchildren,
I curse you for ever.

All those men, women, children and llamas were sacrificed to the gods. In return they asked the gods to protect them and care for them.

The gods let them down.

INCREDIBLE INCAS

GRISLY QUIZ

Now find out if you're a incredible Inca expert!

CRAZY CUSTOMS

The Incans had some batty beliefs and puzzling practices, from harming llamas to making their heads pointy, but which of the following curious customs do you think are true and which are false?

1. The emperor Pachacuti would only eat from golden plates.

2. Inca men were allowed to marry their sisters.

3. The Inca believed that the smaller your earlobes the more important you were.

4. The Incas treated childhood fevers by bathing the baby in wee.

5. The money used by the Incas was made of copper.

6. The Incas' preferred method of transport was the llama.

7. Incans believed it was a great honour to sacrifice their kids to the gods.

8. The Incas cremated their dead after three days.

Ruthless Rulers

The early Inca rulers were a crazy, cut-throat, conquering bunch. Can you match these loopy lords with their claim to fame?

1. Manco Capac
2. Sinchi Roca
3. Lloque Yupanqui
4. Mayta Capac
5. Capac Yupanqui
6. Inca Roca
7. Yahuar Huacac
8. Viracocha

a) Being the ugliest Inca lord ever
b) Being a woeful warrior in the war against the Ayarmarca
c) Being the first Inca lord to be mummified
d) Being a 'Creator God'
e) Being the first Inca lord to capture lands outside the Cuzco Valley
f) Being the first Inca lord
g) Being a beastly bigamist (having a number of wives)
h) Being the biggest, baddest Inca bully

Painful for Peruvians

Life was tough in the Inca Empire – rituals were rough, work was worrisome and if you broke the law or upset the emperor punishments were very painful indeed. Find out what life was like for the incredible Incas with this quick quiz.

1. What did Inca emperor Pachacuti do to his brother when he grew too powerful and popular among the people?
a) Banished him to become a llama farmer
b) Murdered him
c) Had him locked up for the rest of his life

2. Which of the following was not part of the Inca manhood initiation ceremony?
a) Having to whip yourself
b) Having your ears pierced
c) Eating a llama's heart

3. What punishment did Chosen Women suffer if they got pregnant?
a) They and their families were hanged
b) They were buried alive
c) They were forced to sacrifice the child to the gods

4. How were naughty schoolchildren punished?
a) They were caned across the soles of the feet
b) They were given 12 lashes on the back
c) They were made to sleep with the llamas for a week

5. What was the punishment for murder in Inca society?
a) Being thrown off a cliff
b) Being trampled by llamas
c) Hanging

6. What was the punishment for cuddling the emperor's wives?
a) Having your feet chopped off and your eyes gouged out
b) Being fed to the llamas
c) Being stripped naked, tied to a wall and starved to death

7. What did the Incans do with the bones of people executed as witches or wizards?
a) They made them into musical instruments
b) They made them into spoons
c) They were given to the llamas to gnaw on

8. How did the Incans treat a headache?
a) By drinking a mixture made of bark from the pepper tree
b) By gouging out a hole in their head
c) With two aspirin and an early night

LIVE LIKE AN INCA

Everyone had roles and responsibilities in Inca villages and towns, even the llamas. How much have you learned about the day-to-day life in the Inca Empire?

1. What was the *chasqui* chain? (Clue: Get the message?)

2. What did Inca women over 50 do? (Clue: *We'ave* covered this already…)

3. What did Inca women use to hold their hair in place instead of hairspray? (Clue: A strange kind of toiletry)

4. What were Incas over the age of 80 expected to do? (Clue: Oh come on – it's dead easy!)

5. What did the Incas use to make fire when there wasn't any wood? (Clue: An a-llama-ing habit)

6. Which part of the emperor did the Incans offer to the gods after he had died? (Clue: Eye–eye)

7. What did the lucky white llama get to drink in the ceremony to honour Napa? (Clue: Can you *beer* to find out?)

8. Who was the Incan sun-god? (Clue: His name means 'my father')

Crazy Customs
1. True. Crazy Pach believed he was related to the sun god Inti and demanded the greatest luxuries.
2. False. Only the Inca emperor was allowed to marry his sister – it was meant to keep the royal blood pure.
3. False. They believed the BIGGER your ears were the more important you were – and they'd wear huge ear-plugs to stretch their ears.
4. True. They also made the baby drink the wee (would you want to knock back a glass of your little brother's widdle?)
5. False. The Incas didn't use money – they would work for anything they wanted.
6. False. They never rode on the llamas (which were hopeless as horses).
7. True. They thought killing the kids was a fair exchange for the sun and the rain that the gods provided.
8. False. The Incas preferred mummification and burial to cremation. That way they would make it to the afterlife.

Ruthless Rulers
1f; 2c; 3a; 4h; 5e; 6b; 7g; 8d

Painful for Peruvians
1b; 2c; 3b; 4a; 5a; 6c; 7a; 8b

Live like an Inca
1. The relay runners who carried messages across the Inca empire
2. They wove cloth to make clothes
3. Their own wee

4. Nothing – no one lived that long
5. Llama droppings (those llamas came in very handy!)
6. His eyebrows!
7. The Incan beer called chichi

8. Inti (father ... sun ... geddit?!)

INTERESTING INDEX

Where will you find 'frog soup', 'llama droppings' and 'showing backsides' in an index? In a Horrible Histories book, of course!

Terry Deary was born at a very early age, so long ago he can't remember. But his mother, who was there at the time, says he was born in Sunderland, north-east England, in 1946 – so it's not true that he writes all *Horrible Histories* from memory. At school he was a horrible child only interested in playing football and giving teachers a hard time. His history lessons were so boring and so badly taught, that he learned to loathe the subject. *Horrible Histories* is his revenge.

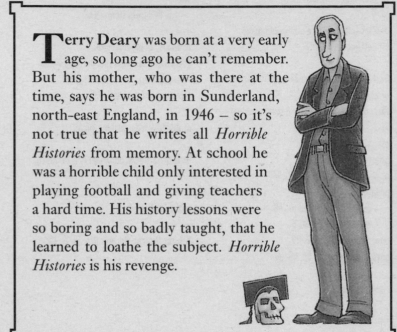